Turning Grief into Gratitude

Turning Grief

A Paper Spider Production
Ottawa, Canada

What readers are saying . . .

"**R**abbi Reuven Bulka stands out for his combination of profound commitment to, and knowledge of Judaism, a deep understanding of psychology, and a truly extraordinary capacity for human empathy. They all coalesce in this book, *Turning Grief into Gratitude*."

—*Dennis Prager, Nationally syndicated radio talk show host, recipient of the American Jewish Press Association's Award for Excellence in Commentary, author of* Happiness Is a Serious Problem *and three other books*

"**I**n a respectful and compassionate manner [Rabbi Bulka] skillfully leads you through the mourning process using his personal experience as the guide."

—*Jim Orban, Publisher of* The Ottawa Citizen

"**A** thoughtful and sensitive book . . . a rabbi and psychologist, he [Rabbi Bulka] offers keen insight on how to deal with death and mourning and how to offer proper consolation to those who have lost loved ones. This is a touching and helpful volume."

—*Rabbi Marc D. Angel, Spiritual Leader of Congregation Shearith Israel, and Author of* Foundations of Sephardic Spirituality

"**M**ost helpful to all of us who feel awkward during times of grief."

—*Brian McGarry, CEO, McGarry Family Chapels*

What readers are saying ...

"**What** a wonderful fulfillment of the Fifth Commandment. Rabbi Reuven Bulka has written a stirring and loving portrait of two remarkable people, his own mother and father. *Turning Grief into Gratitude* is filled with interesting anecdotes and wisdom. You leave the book understanding why Rabbi Hayyim Yaakov and Rebbetzin Yehudis Bulka have been such enduring role models in the lives of their children."

— *Rabbi Joseph Telushkin, Author of* A Code of Jewish Ethics, *and* Jewish Literacy

"**Rabbi** Bulka has used his wonderful sense of humour, his personal story of grief, his many years of experience as a rabbi comforting mourners, and his scholarly appraisal of experts to help us understand what mourners truly need so that we can help them on their journey."

— *Hartley Stern M.D., Professor of Surgery, University of Ottawa, Vice-President Cancer Program, Ottawa Hospital*

"**An** invaluable guide ... Readers who will find this work of tremendous benefit include people who are mourning or comforting a mourner ... "

— *Rabbi Levi Meier, Ph.D., Chaplain/Psychologist, Cedars-Sinai Medical Center*

More endorsements on page 8 ...

into Gratitude

Reflections and Recommendations
on Mourning and Condolence

Rabbi Dr. Reuven P. Bulka
Foreword by Rabbi Maurice Lamm

Attention corporations, associations, and organizations: Enjoy 40% off and use our books as fund-raisers, premiums, or gifts. Phone *Paper Spider* at 1-888-BOOKS-88 (1-888-266-5788) or 613-321-9850 to arrange.

For school libraries and charitable organizations: Learn more about our *Special Donations Program* and *Free Books for School Libraries Program* on our web site at

http://www.PaperSpider.Net/about/

Printed in Canada

Cover design: Claude Cheung
www.ClaudeCheung.com

Library and Archives Canada Cataloguing in Publication

Bulka, Reuven P.
    Turning grief into gratitude : reflections and recommendations on mourning and condolence / Reuven P. Bulka.

Includes bibliographical references.
ISBN 0-9732523-6-7 (pbk.)

    1. Grief--Religious aspects--Judaism. 2. Bereavement--Religious aspects--Judaism. I. Title.

BM645.G74B86 2006   296.7   C2006-905414-2

Dedication

For my sister *Rivka* and my niece *Tova*

whose care for my parents
was beyond extraordinary

"Rabbi Bulka's book, *Turning Grief into Gratitude,* is an intensely personal account of, and set of reflections on his own processes of mourning. Both the narrative and the commentary are highly nuanced, subtle, wise—and moving in their directness and simplicity."

—*Aviva Freedman, Professor of Linguistics and Applied Language Studies, Carleton University*

"This book is comforting and informative with a gift for everyone."

—*Dawn Brown, International Speaker & Author of* That Perception Thing!

"He [Rabbi Bulka] provides insights into the true essence of supporting those who are grieving."

—*Michael Allen, President & CEO, United Way-Centraide Ottawa*

"... a sensitive portrayal of the importance of family values and tradition in a world where these are too often forgotten."

—*Dr. Jack Kitts, President & CEO, The Ottawa Hospital*

Contents

Photos

Foreword by Rabbi Maurice Lamm

Best-selling Author of
The Jewish Way in Death and Mourning

There are books that are too complicated or simple, stuffy or light, complex or simplistic. There also are books, more uncommonly, that are both sweet and thoughtful, and their authors are admired for what their writings reveal about their characters. *Turning Grief into Gratitude* by Rabbi Dr. Reuven P. Bulka is that kind of book—sweet and thoughtful, and written by a delightful and intelligent person.

The book is heartwarming, exceptional in this arena of literature, and you could feel the reader's envy of someone having such parents, although I have been blessed as he has been. The uncomplicated, open, all-loving embrace of son and parents informs every paragraph, can be sensed effortlessly, and its honey clings to every page even when the topic changes. So, it is an appealing and warm book. You feel good reading it. What more does a reader need?

A reader needs substance. Fortunately, *Turning Grief into Gratitude* is also very thoughtful. Here you have an honest writer, who is a Ph.D., a Jewish scholar, and a dedicated and loyal rabbi who cares for his flock as a shepherd should. That he is honest is evident at every turn of a phrase, as for example, when he is critical of well-meaning but unthinking well-wishers. In my own recent book, *Consolations,* I dedicated a large chapter to "Words for a Loss, When at a Loss for Words," because the consoling platitudes were clogging my eardrums and stifling my imagination. And, as Rabbi Bulka notes, the platitudes don't compare to the peccadilloes that are pronounced as received wisdom from Sinai.

The author, who has written his thesis on Logotherapy and Viktor Frankl, demonstrates profound sensitivity to the bruised emotions of all recent mourners, and readers would do well to follow his cautionary advice and consent to stop and think before they enter a *shiv'ah* house (house of mourning).

In the interest of the full disclosure policy of the American corporate establishment, I hereby notify all readers that my granddaughter is married to the author's son. But I assure you that this information did not prejudice the above thoughts, so much as it enabled me to write with a facile pen and a steady hand about a subject and a person I know well.

Buy the book; you'll like it.

Maurice Lamm

Acknowledgements

Growing up, family time was Friday night. Part of the Friday night protocol was to separate the eating of the fish and the meat with a little wine. (Consuming fish and meat together is prohibited by Jewish Law for health reasons, so separating with a drink is necessary.) Since this is a health-related imbibe, we accompany the drinking with the word *L'Hayyim*, literally "To Life."

On occasion, when it seemed like a toast had already been proposed, and was now being proposed a second time, I would respond not with *"L'Hayyim,"* but with a curt "I said it already."

My parents would point out that it is easier to say *"L'Hayyim"* (one word) than "I said it already" (four words). That lesson remains deeply imbedded within me, even as I thank—again—my sister, Rivka, and my niece Tova for the loving care they extended to my parents. That *thank you* permeates this book, and even though "I said it already" in the book, it is still important to say it again in the Acknowledgements.

Thanks to all those who were so vital a part of my parents' lives—the family, the friends, the colleagues, the congregants, the students. Many people were deeply involved in their lives, yet a few stand out for the extraordinary care they extended in the later years. They are Dr. Doron Spierer, Sandy and Gloria Kestenbaum, Dr. Barrie Kaufman, and Dr. David Stein.

I am grateful to my respected colleagues for their kind approbations. One in particular, Dr. Aviva Freedman, made some invaluable suggestions that have been incorporated in the book.

The gracious Foreword by Rabbi Maurice Lamm, himself a most inspiring teacher and role model, is a most welcome enhancement of this volume.

The people who run *Paper Spider*, Bina Ester and Yankl Botwinik, took on this project as a labor of love, and nurtured it through with amazing attention to every detail and nuance. The final product is a tribute to their expertise and dedication.

Finally, I thank my dear wife, Leah, for reading the manuscript many times, making helpful suggestions, and spending many hours going over my parents' papers in Jerusalem. She knew my parents for only a short time, but connected with them almost immediately on a most profound level.

In their life together, my parents inspired so many. In this book, I aspire to offer this inspiration on the altar of posterity, as a way of perpetuating their lives.

Introduction

Ever
notice how children
speak about their departed parents
with smiles on their faces? These are the
same children who cried and mourned when
their parents died. How do we account for this trans-
formation? How and when does grief turn into gratitude?
How does intense sorrow give way to appreciation for a
full life? There is no simple answer to this question. We each
go through this journey at our own pace, consistent with our
own make-up and prior life experiences. But at some point in
time, this change of attitude does take place, or at least it
should take place. Otherwise, the mourners may remain
mired in perpetual melancholy. This book is a chronicle
of sorts, of a journey from grief to gratitude. It is a
journey that I took recently and share with you
here. It is the story of my parents, and of the
mourning toward appreciation that I
experienced. My parents, Rabbi
Hayyim Yaakov

(Jacob) and Rebbetzin Yehudis (Eda) Bulka, lived an exemplary life together on many levels. They endured the challenges of their early years together; they raised their children, Rivka, Yitzchok, and me (I am the middle child) together; they served their congregational community together; they re-established themselves in Jerusalem together; they lovingly nurtured an entire generation of grandchildren and great-grandchildren together; they fought through illness together; and they died almost together.

My father died on the second day of Adar 5766, corresponding to March 1, 2006. My mother died on the second day of Nisan 5766, corresponding to March 30, 2006.

In Judaism, the basic period of mourning is thirty days, called the *sheloshim* (literally, thirty). The period of mourning for a parent is a full year, an extension of the thirty days out of deference to the parents.

Parents may absolve children from keeping the year of mourning, but not the *sheloshim*. The *sheloshim* is the sum total of the seven-day intense mourning period called *shiv'ah* (literally, seven) and the balance of twenty-three days. If parents do so instruct, the children remain obligated nonetheless.

All this is by way of sharing the significance of my mother's passing on the last day of the thirty-day mourning period for my father. No one knows anything about the inner motivations and wishes that may have been at work in my mother's heart, but the fact is that my mother did not intrude for even a moment on my father's mourning period. Though she died thirty days later, it is fair to say that my parents died together, albeit at different times.

What follows herein is a mix of personal reflections on the life of my parents, and a retrospective on the grieving process. The first part focuses on the actual days of their passing. In the second part, I reflect on the many childhood memories that invariably come to the fore when parents pass away. The third part concentrates on the extraordinary memories left by my parents, memories that evoke a strong feeling of admiration. In the fourth part, I share observations on the mourning process, and in the fifth on the challenging obligation to comfort mourners.

There is much to be learned from my parents' life, and much to be learned from the aftermath, including how grief turns into appreciation.

Ultimately, this metamorphosis is in the hands of each mourner; however, there is so much that others can do to help this development along. The right way of comforting is of inestimable value. Sending the right message, saying the right words, doing the right thing, all help the mourner to move almost unconsciously from crying to smiling, from lamenting "Why" to saying "Thank You" to God for the great blessings bestowed.

In the journey I share with you, the move from grief to gratitude was helped along by a combination of circumstance, of comforting by others, and of reflection on two wonderful and intertwined lives. Even though every situation is unique, I hope that this chronicle helps others who face the almost inevitable loss of parents and other loved ones.

May this all help to perpetuate the vibrant memory of my parents.

Reuven P. Bulka

Chapter One

The Dreaded Day

"Usually death is compared with sleep. Actually, however, dying should be compared with being wakened. At least this comparison makes it comprehensible that death is beyond comprehension."

—Viktor E. Frankl

In my capacity as president of an international rabbinic organization, I was scheduled to be in Israel from February 27 to March 2, 2006, for this group's yearly conference based in Jerusalem. My dear sister, Rivka (I always called her that, though her friends call her Rebecca), came at the same time, from her home in Edison, New Jersey, just to look in on my parents, as she did so often, and to address the latest series of challenges as they unfolded.

As events dictated, I spent relatively little time at the conference. My father was not well, and was getting worse. The past year, and specifically the past few months, was an emotional roller coaster, with close calls and miraculous quasi-recoveries.

Dad was enduring excruciating pain and was unable to sleep.

Dr. Doron Spierer, a precious and devoted man, came every night to check on him. We all agreed that it was unwise to put Dad through this agony and that we should try to alleviate the pain, even though this would make him drowsy and less alert to the world — something that he dreaded.

A light dose of morphine seemed to do the trick, and my father had a calm night. Nevertheless, the next day brought more pain, and another check-in by the good doctor, who again, with my father's agreement and insistence on only a light dose, gave him a very small amount of morphine.

We left that night with Dad seemingly resting comfortably. It turned out to be false comfort. The next morning, Rivka was awakened early by Revi, the person looking after my parents, with very sad news. My sister called me immediately and began with two powerful words: "It's over."

Considering that I had still not changed my plans to return home to Ottawa after the conference as scheduled, this came as a shock, but not a great one. No one articulated it, but we knew that it was only a matter of time, that the many health deficits that my father had been fighting would eventually overpower him.

As Dr. Spierer had put it, "Right now we are fighting the continual emergencies with antibiotics. But one day something will come up and we will not have the ammunition to fight."

My father died, but not without a heroic struggle. There was no time to sit down and cry, because from the moment we found out, around 6:30 in the morning Jerusalem time, we were pressed into action to ensure that the funeral would take place that day. That is the Jewish way, to drop everything and to focus exclusively on attending to the deceased and making all the necessary arrangements.

The Burial Society, known as the Hevra Kadisha, came within a few hours to take my father to Eretz HaHayyim, a cemetery outside Bet Shemesh (about a half-hour drive from Jerusalem), which had become the site of our family plots. There, my father was prepared with the usual meticulous dignity for the funeral at 2 PM, only eight hours after he breathed his last. In Israel, this is not unusual.

In these eight hours, we had to notify everyone, place signs with funeral details in strategic places in the neighborhood where my father lived (signs which, in Jerusalem, are made in the space of a few minutes), hire a bus to take people to and from the funeral, prepare an appropriate and befitting service and eulogies, and look after other funeral-related details, including arrangements to care for my mother, who was not well enough to attend her own husband's funeral.

The accent in all this was on doing that which would bestow the full dignity and honor on my father that he so richly deserved.

We left for the funeral still pre-occupied with ensuring that all the arrangements were in place, and with anxiety about the unsettling situation of my mother, whose condition we had thought more precarious than my father's.

We went to the funeral reflecting on some of the many highlights of Dad's life, and upset by the fact that Mom was not able to really apprehend what had happened.

We knew that many people would not find out about the funeral in time and would be upset. For that reason, among others, it was only right to have a memorial for my father at the conclusion of the thirty-day period when the gravesite monument would be dedicated. So, not long after our return home that day, we set the date for this memorial and were able to share it with everyone who came to offer condolence.

During the *shiv'ah*, our attention was very much on Mom. We were prepared for anything, but my mother hung on. Even as we were inching closer to the memorial for my father, slated for March 28, we were not sure whether this memorial would actually take place. If Mom did not make it through to then, obviously the mourning for her would have pre-empted a memorial for my father.

The day after the memorial for my father, I flew to New York on my return trip to Ottawa for the Sabbath. I was very much aware of the life hanging in the balance, but Mom, in her quiet way, was quite tenacious, strong of heart, refusing to surrender.

And, truth be told, I hated the idea of staying on in Israel for a deathwatch, waiting for my mother to die. I simply could not bear that thought. It struck me as totally antithetical to the basic wish that we have for our parents to live, even though my mother by this time was not really conscious and aware.

My sister had booked to stay for a longer period, so she remained in Israel. As soon as I landed in New York, my sister, Dr. Spierer and I were in communication. Dr. Spierer knew of my parents' resilience and had become quite reluctant to make predictions. Yet, this time, he was pessimistic and surmised that we were dealing with perhaps a few more hours. He urged me to return, as did my sister. Thankfully, I was able to get a return flight to Israel almost immediately, which got me there by early Friday morning. When I landed, I learned that Mom had passed away while I was in flight.

Had I not made the plane, I would have missed my mother's funeral on Friday, since the funeral would not have been delayed until Sunday. In fact, even if the funeral were scheduled for Sunday, I still would have missed it due to the time differential between the East Coast and Israel, and the prohibition against taking a plane on the holy Sabbath.

By the time I arrived, most of the funeral arrangements were already in place. Because the funeral took place on a Friday, when everyone is rushing to prepare for the Sabbath, we thought relatively few people would attend. We were wrong. My mother had many admirers, and they made a special effort to pay tribute to her. The chapel was packed for her, as it had been for my father.

Looking back, both funerals gave me the strange sensation of an out-of-body experience. I felt that I was somewhat in a trance and things were happening as if on a runaway freight train, with very little control on my part. It was like something I was watching, even though it was happening to me and to my family.

🪷

The passing of my parents was, and remains, a great loss.

The mourning period for my parents was a busy time, with limited opportunity to reflect on their lives. This book is a partial redress of that deficit, in that much of the contemplation of their lives is happening now as I write, and as I share with you the story of two remarkable lives.

Both my parents escaped from Nazi tentacles. When my grandparents saw the storm clouds starting to hover over Germany, they sent my father away from Nuremberg. My father came to England on his own, around the age of thirteen, and was able to continue his studies, eventually receiving *semikhah* (rabbinic ordination).

Some of his letters to his parents, though he was not even sure they were reaching their destination, were full of faith and hope and trepidation. That was faith at a very young age.

My mother likewise was sent away from Stettin, Germany, to England. Her family tells me that she too was imbued with faith from her childhood, and they recall quite vividly her adherence to faith and her leadership qualities. That faith undoubtedly carried each of them through those dark years of separation from their parents.

In England, my parents met through the suggestion of the Presler family, who gave domicile to my mother. They married and became a team for the better part of 64 years. They were supremely devoted to each other and were a quiet but effective model for marital togetherness.

For thirty-three years, they were a potent rabbinic duo, working together to build and maintain a most appreciative community in the Bronx, New York. When they moved to Jerusalem, they wove their rabbinic magic with similar energy on an equally appreciative community, though they did all this for a much smaller salary, namely zero.

My father had always been the model of what a rabbi should be, and he set the standard, which I try to follow, though it is impossible to replicate. To follow almost always means that you do not catch up. In this instance, the standard is so high that catch-up is not even a remote possibility.

A few months after my parents' passing, my wife Leah and I went to Israel for the sole purpose of putting my parents' house in order. We went through the myriad files that Dad kept. He retained everything, including all the letters we sent to my parents from camp to all the report cards. There were hundreds of letters from deeply appreciative congregants and non-congregants that testified to the meticulous care my father gave to everyone. The sheer magnitude of the gratitude was overwhelming and a further reminder of how replication of the Rabbi Jacob Bulka rabbinic way is beyond the realm of the possible.

He and I had talked often about rabbinic matters, and Dad loved to hear all the goings-on in my life as a congregational leader. He soaked it all in, and often remembered what I told him better than I did.

Mourning is somewhat narcissistic, in that we focus on what the loss of a family member or friend means to us, the bereft survivors. For me, it means that my children will no longer be able to reap from the inspiration and love that my parents shared so generously and so energetically with us over the years. It means, as well, that I will not be able to share happenings and good news with my parents.

This all hit home when I received a call from the President of Carleton University, a premier educational institution in Canada's capital, during the mourning period after the passing of my parents. The President, Dr. David Atkinson, asked if I would agree to receive an honorary doctorate from Carleton University and to deliver the commencement address.

He must still be wondering why I did not respond immediately and say *yes*. I was not sure whether it was appropriate to accept such an honor during the mourning period for my parents. I stalled by joking a bit with him, he being such a congenial person. During that time, I was thinking about my parents, how on the other hand, this would have been such a wondrous moment for them. I went through a quick debate about whether to go ahead during this period of mourning or to wait for the next graduation.

However, knowing how much both my father and my mother would have delighted in this honor pushed me over the line, and I said *yes*. After telling my wife, calling my parents would have been the first thing on the agenda. But I could not.

This is a great regret. But a regret is not a complaint. Regret is no more a complaint than is sadness a manifestation of anger.

Little Reuven 7½ months & little Rivka 1¾ years old

Chapter Two

Childhood Memories

It is too bad that we only become wise as we mature, if at all. In the early years, we do not appreciate our parents as much as we appreciate them later on. Or at least the appreciation is on a more material level. In the early years we look upon our parents as our providers, hardly apprehending the impact they make on the outside world. In the childhood years, one's inner world is the only world that exists.

For me, that inner world reflected an old-world parenting style. There were no free rides. If we under-achieved, that would not go unnoticed. I remember report card time as trauma time, because there, on that cardboard, would be the record of my grades, my effort, and my behavior.

I was far from being a model child. My grades were at times not up to par, and I often incurred the wrath of my parents for not living up to my ability. One time, I flunked math. My parents were angry with me; in retrospect, understandably so. They bought none of my excuses. They insisted I do better. I studied hard to improve, to the point that for the next term, I received the highest grade in the class.

I even started to like math, which I had hated when flunking. It was to become somewhat of a flirtation, in that I started off college by declaring math as my major. I soon realized that my old dislike of math was the real me, that psychology was more consistent with my interests, so I switched majors in mid-stream.

My parents were from the old school. They never bought into the "my child is always right and the teacher is always wrong" attitude. If a teacher would call to say that I was misbehaving, they believed the teacher, not me. I protested then, but I realize that they were right, because I really was misbehaving. Precisely because of their prodding, I graduated as valedictorian for my class. It was really their valedictory, not mine.

I am vehemently anti-smoking. People ask me if I ever smoked. I say yes, and they appreciate my vehemence, until

I tell them the other part of the response — yes, when I was nine years old.

This will give you an idea of how mischievous I was. It has been called the RK syndrome, being a Rabbi's Kid, always in a fish bowl and wanting out in a big way. That this is what precipitated my misbehavior is entirely possible, though being an RK has many advantages, especially if people like and respect the rabbi as much as they liked and respected my father and mother. These feelings are transferred over to the children.

Back to the smoking. When I was nine, cigarette smoking was a big taboo for kids. It was then what drugs are today. But rascal me wanted to indulge in this big taboo. So, I arranged with a contemporary to smoke a cigarette, which I think I took from my father's stash. We chose the bathroom in the synagogue where my father was the rabbi, a stupid nine-year-old's choice. But we had no other place.

We were caught, not by the police, but by a member of the congregation who was a good friend of my parents. He was so angry with me that he threatened to tell my parents. I knew that would be disastrous for me, so I pleaded with him not to tell. I was trembling with fear.

He offered a brilliant compromise. If I would promise never to smoke again, he would not tell my parents. I had no choice. I promised, and he never told, I think. My parents never mentioned anything, and I have kept this promise. This fine gentleman is no longer alive, so I guess I am in the clear; however, I have no intention of ever smoking.

I once mentioned that someone had come around to the school announcing an essay contest. I had brushed it off, being all of nine years old, but my mother, who always wanted the best for me, and encouraged me to exert myself to the best of my ability, insisted that I submit an essay.

An added stress to my already full day of school and homework was not what I relished, especially since it would compromise my ability to follow baseball. However, there was no escaping the directive of my mother.

When I found out the parameters of the essay, I was even more upset. I had to read about a topic and then write an essay. Imagine, I had to read a long book and then put thoughts together. I picked the shortest book, read it very slowly since it was so boring, and then wrote my essay. It was about the great Cantor Yossele Rosenblatt, whom I learned to admire as I matured.

I was greatly relieved to finish the essay and hand it in. Months later, out of the blue, some stranger came into our class to announce the results of the essay contest. I had long forgotten about it and was not really tuned in, since I was sure that the winner came from another school.

I was shocked to hear him say that I had won the contest. First prize was five more books. No big deal. *Winning* was a big deal, because it would make Mom happy. And it did.

I found out a bit later that my victory was not such a triumph. I was the only one to submit an essay! I did not have the heart to tell Mom, and to this day I have no idea why it took the judges four months to read the only essay. I guess this was the beginning of my writing, for which I thank my mother.

Pre-teen Reuven

My parents wanted the best for us, but they also wanted the best *from* us. In this, they were insistent. Laziness, haphazard application, lack of cooperation had no place in their aspirations for us. It is not easy for parents to be strict disciplinarians as well as affectionate when having to deal with children like me, so I received lots of discipline and enough affection.

A good example of how my parents combined the two occurred just after my becoming Bar Mitzvah, old enough to be counted in a *minyan* (quorum) and lead services.

One time, the person who regularly read the weekly Biblical excerpt on the Sabbath was unexpectedly called away. Dad was desperate to get someone to replace him. He asked me if I could do it and, as an inducement, promised that I could go to a baseball game on the Friday afternoon at Yankee Stadium if I had mastered the reading by then.

I was then an avid baseball fan and was excited enough about this to sacrifice the hours it would take. The fateful test would come on Thursday evening, when my father would listen to me. I could read from the text with the vowels, but not from the other side of the page, which had no punctuation and was like the actual Torah scroll from which I would need to read on the Sabbath — a much more daunting challenge.

To put it bluntly, I faked it. I was not ready, but I read from the side with the vowels and pretended that I was reading from the difficult side. My father was satisfied. I had pulled off this great trick, and off to the game I went on Friday.

Nevertheless, I knew I was in trouble if I goofed up on the Sabbath at the public reading. So, after the game (which the Yankees lost 4–2; trivial things sometimes stand out), I came home and, after the Sabbath meal, stayed up the entire night to master the reading.

My parents, to their eternal credit, forgot most of my childhood nonsense, but I do not forget. And I appreciate even more how they guided me in those early years, with firmness and with great confidence in my ability, which they expressed merely by insisting that I could do better.

Rabbi Dad

I have vague and sporadic recollections of my early years, but the perspective of time gives some meaning to those recollections.

I remember the time that my father applied for the position of Rabbi of Congregation Khal Adath Yeshurun, at that time one of the leading congregations situated in Bronx, New York.

The chance that an untested novice would be chosen for this position, a position that attracted applications from a huge number of rabbis, was remote, to say the least.

My father had the requisite rabbinic degree, but no real formal experience. I recall some of my parents' conversations at home. Rivka and I learned more from making believe we were not listening. We heard about how the chances were minimal, that as exciting as this position promised to be, it was not to be.

Then came the unexpected ecstasy of being chosen. It was an electric moment in the house. Looking back, I fully understand why the selection committee for the synagogue chose my father. They must have been impressed with his fiery oratory, combined with a heavy but refined British accent, and completely bowled over by his personality, which undoubtedly they found irresistible.

What made little sense then, makes eminent sense now. This is just one of many examples, examples of how childhood memories help one to gain a more complete understanding with the benefit of time and the wisdom of hindsight.

I walked to shul (synagogue) with Dad every Sabbath morning. It was a short walk of one long block. On one of these walks, we saw a man walking away from the synagogue. When he saw my father, he took out a *kippah* (head covering, also known as *yarmulkah,* meaning awe of the Majesty) and placed it on his head. As he approached my father and nodded his wishes, he was appropriately attired with this head covering.

My father kept on walking toward the synagogue, and I kept pace but looked back to see if that person still had the head covering on. He did not.

At the time, I thought it was somewhat bizarre that a person who knows of the importance of the *kippah* would take it off so quickly. With the benefit of hindsight, I realize that he had great respect for my father, as did so many others, and this was his way of showing it. What was bizarre then is no longer so quirky.

Having been chosen to lead this large congregation had its down side. Dad was hardly home during our childhood years. Thank God for the Sabbath. That was when we all connected as a family. Nevertheless, my father was busy during the week. We missed his presence, but we never complained. We knew that he was not out on the town. I realize now how much he achieved during those years.

He was deeply immersed in every facet of the Bronx community's welfare. He was instrumental in establishing the community *eruv* (Sabbath boundary creating an enclosed area within which carrying is permissible, an activity which is otherwise forbidden on the Sabbath). He was a vital part of the rabbinic team that maintained the kosher (ritual acceptability of food items) standards in the community. He actively helped people find appropriate employment.

He was *everywhere*. He did all the rabbi things, in his own unique style. When he visited a family during a mourning period, he was totally there. It was never a five-minute pit stop. His visits combined the fullness of time with the fullness of concentration — caring that was matchless. He spent hours fixing marriages that were on the brink of collapse.

My father was a leading rabbi in the community. He was respected as much for his selflessness as for his wisdom.

One rabbi who chaired a most vital national rabbinic body told me that fractious fighting was the normal order of the day for the regular meetings of that group. He always breathed a sigh of relief when my father came, because he knew that my father's presence calmed the atmosphere and allowed the meeting to go on with less cantankerousness.

He was the ultimate team player. Had he possessed a big ego, he would easily have become the titular head of many a group. As it is, he chaired many an organization, but only after he was begged to assume such a position.

As I grew older, I started to spend more time at the synagogue. Age has its privileges, including a later evening curfew. I was allowed to attend the daily evening services, which in the summer could end quite late.

There were always meetings going on, and I would wait to go home with Dad. But there was a major problem. If there was anyone who needed a lift home, guess who was the driver? This was almost a daily ritual. It was a rare and welcome occasion when we drove straight home from the synagogue.

My father had a habit, which, in my formative and cranky years, was just short of maddening. When he took someone home, he insisted on taking that person to the door. A house away was not good enough. Even if taking someone right to the door necessitated a major detour around one-way streets, that is the way it was.

Nothing stood in my father's way. No amount of complaining by yours truly could deter him from this course. Nor did the entreaties of the benefactors of my father's kindness ever succeed in getting him to let them off a bit away from the target.

What was upsetting then is now recalled with great pride in my father's way. He never did anything half-baked. He insisted that if you are going to do a kindness, do it without compromise. That way you show that you really want to do it. The way my father did kindness gave the impression that *he* was the benefactor. He appreciated being given the opportunity to do a good deed.

A 'Moving' Episode

The episode that stands out most in my mind took place in my early teens.

We were driving to our new home on West Farms Road, which was now a bit further from the synagogue. As we were approaching an available parking spot on the street — which was always a happy discovery — Dad experienced massive chest pains. He was in such excruciating pain, he almost doubled over and was hardly able to move any part of his body. We were to learn later that he had suffered a nearly fatal heart attack. The treatment prescribed for him at that time was strict bed rest for six months. No work at all.

Back to the parking. It took my father's last bit of energy to park the car, a large pink Mercury with no power steering. We all got out to make our way home. On the way, Dad looked back and did not like what he saw. He had parked in a way that inadvertently took up two spots.

We begged him to go on home, but he refused. He dragged himself back to the Mercury, got in, and moved the car forward so that a full parking space became available behind his car.

Needless to say, we were upset with him. How could he be so oblivious to the emergency that was exploding inside him?! With the perspective of time, I now understand. Admittedly, I would not recommend a similar action to anyone faced with such a circumstance, but this was my father in full relief.

He could not swallow the thought that he had been uncaring about others, even if the issue was something trivial like a parking spot, even if the person disadvantaged by his action was a stranger whom he would probably never meet. All that did not matter. What mattered was to be an unconditionally caring person at all times, even in times of personal crisis, even if no one would ever find out about the caring.

This is a powerful remembrance of my father. Its message transmits his usual "do as you see" approach, rather than the much less effective "do as I tell you."

Transplantation

The massive coronary that my father suffered came at a most demanding time in his rabbinic life. The synagogue that he led was as imposing as ever. The neighborhood was deteriorating. People were moving away out of fear, as street taunting and insult were becoming a daily occurrence. A nearly empty *shul*, which was once full and housed a thousand people, is a dreary and depressing sight.

My father could have walked away by selling the *shul* and pocketing a deserved sum for retirement, in recognition of his dedicated service for about two decades. Other rabbis in similar situations did just that.

My father refused to hear of this. The congregation had a distinguished legacy, and he was not about to let that legacy go down the drain. He mobilized the congregation to relocate the synagogue to a better area, so that its legacy could continue.

For a few taxing years, my father oversaw the building of a new edifice at the same time that he took care of the slowly dying old synagogue. In the middle of summer, he would walk from East Bronx to Pelham Parkway, a walk of at least three miles, in the sweltering New York heat and humidity.

Though he had lots of help from a dedicated group of supporters, the burden fell primarily on my father. It is no surprise that this herculean responsibility nearly killed him. However, it would have been futile to argue with him. The best evidence that this is true is the fact that after recovering from the heart attack, he went back to assuming the burden of two congregations. When Dad made up his mind about anything, there was nothing that could convince him otherwise.

I am sure that he did not think that his insistence on returning to work was risky. We were worried, but he was confident he could handle it, otherwise he would not have jeopardized his wife and family. I remember complaining to his doctor at the time, but he reassured our family that if my father overstepped, the body would send the appropriate signal.

Looking back to when Dad was in his mid-forties, our gratitude is compounded by the realization that we almost lost him then. As much as his dogged determination made little sense to us then, in retrospect it was vintage my father, another instance of showing what made him who he was. When I mentioned that his is a rabbinic calling that is impossible to replicate, you can better appreciate the accuracy of this observation.

Ironically, this health crisis was the key factor in determining my own career. I had visions of becoming a doctor, but all that was put on hold when Dad became ill. Someone had to fill in during his absence, and the congregation did not have the money to hire a replacement. So guess who became the interim fill-in (I don't want to claim that I was the interim "rabbi," since I was still in rabbinical school and far away from ordination).

I got a first-hand taste of the rabbinate, giving speeches and classes, though I was thankfully not asked to officiate at funerals or weddings. And the taste was enough to push me toward a life as a rabbi. It was also the time when my relationship with my father shifted into a higher gear. We were obviously not colleagues, but we also were no longer father and kid. It was now father and more mature son. This is when we began to share so many of the intricacies of being a rabbi.

I still remember the electric feeling in the congregation on the first Sabbath when my father returned to prayer services. He was well enough to come, but not well enough to speak. This was the first time that Dad would actually hear me. Until now, I just shared with him what I had said. I shook in my shoes. And goofed up big time. But Dad was always encouraging.

Thanks to my father, I was able to master the ability to give speeches without notes. That was his way always, and I started out copying his way, relying on the luxury that I could do no wrong since I was so young. Ever since then, when I was sixteen, that has been my way, which was my father's way. By now, I am too old to change.

As an additional irony, the congregation in Ottawa that first hired me was faced with a challenge similar to my father's: a deteriorating neighborhood translating into a nearly empty synagogue. In fact, when I was first interviewed for the position,

I was asked if I would stay long enough to help the congregation relocate. I said that I would, and kept my word. I am still at that congregation, more than thirty years after the move.

The similarities do not carry through beyond the basics. The challenges I faced with the move pale in comparison with those faced by my father, but his inspiration was undoubtedly very much at work in helping effect the move in Ottawa.

Passion

My father was a superb orator, even though he never went to a school of oratory. His speeches were well thought-out, highly involved, and always came back to the starting point, even if you thought that the presentation had veered off course. He had a marvelous sense of humor, and his humor was all the more powerful because it was not something you expected from a man of such scholarship and devotion.

In my frequent walks to *shul* on Sabbath, Dad would complain that he had nothing to say. After a few experiences of this "nothing," I was daring enough to say that I was not worried, that I was sure there would be plenty to say.

"You always say that, but it turns out to be untrue," became my standard retort. Dad would listen, and respond, "But this time I really have nothing!" This went on for years, in fact forever, even after my father left for Jerusalem and talked about the speech that he was about to give. I was reliving my childhood on the telephone from Israel.

Combined with the "nothing" was a great passion. All my father's speeches started low and went up in tempo and pitch to the great crescendo. My father was a passionate champion of Israel and the Jewish people, and had zero tolerance for bigotry and hate. His passion never abated. Even in his later years, I never heard him give a speech that was devoid of passion. (See his caring message to his Congregation prior to moving to Israel, in Appendix A.)

His passion was a driving force in all he did. Sometimes, passion can give way to burnout, but never with my father. The depth of his caring and his genuine love of people never slacked off.

In Israel, my father gave twelve classes a week when he was at his peak, which lasted well into his eighties. When you factor in preparation time, getting there, and getting back, you wonder when he had the time for anything else.

But passion creates time, time to go to every family wedding, to every family Bar and Bat Mitzvah, to the circumcisions of the grandchildren, and to every wedding and joyous event which he was asked to attend and officiate at. We were amazed by the sheer number of people who came to visit during the *shiv'ah* in Jerusalem, well into the hundreds, just to share their gratitude for the extra mile my father went for them.

You would think he was being paid huge sums for all these classes, and he was, but not in dollars. He was being paid in giant doses of joy and fulfillment for being able to teach to students who came in droves and who loved him to the core, as a person and as a teacher.

As his health problems started to gang up on him, my father, as was his lifelong pattern, refused to give in. He continued giving all his classes. Eventually it became impossible for him to continue, so he "slowed down" to only five classes a week; full time for any other mortal, but a big comedown for him.

This slowing down did not come easily. We had many an argument with him, begging him to cut down, to save his strength, but to no avail. Again in hindsight, we now realize even more than before how much these classes were his lifeline, how they energized him even as his strength was waning.

"*Even in advanced years one should not envy a young person. Why should one? For the possibilities a young person has, or for his future? No, I should say that, instead of possibilities in the future, the older person has realities in the past—work done, love loved, and suffering suffered.*"

—*Viktor E. Frankl*

Chapter Three

Appreciating My Parents

My parents were deeply devout. They loved Judaism, they appreciated the Torah, they venerated the sages.

One day, when I was eighteen, I came home and found Dad crying like I had never before seen him cry.

His manifest sobbing, which that day was quite surprising, shocking, even scary, was eminently appropriate. It turned out that my father just found out about the death of one of the great luminaries of his generation, Rabbi Aharon Kotler of Lakewood, widely hailed as the person most responsible for awakening a slumbering America to the importance of

Torah education and building the institutions to make Torah education available to the multitudes.

He was crying at the passing of this great sage as if he had lost his own father. Perhaps Rabbi Kotler was a father figure to my Dad, as he was to so many.

According to my best guess, Dad never experienced the intense seven-day mourning for an immediate family member. He never knew when his parents and his brother died, as they were murdered by the Nazis. And my father passed away before his only surviving sister, and before my mother, so he never sat *shiv'ah*—officially at least.

Having never really mourned for his own father, the mourning for Rabbi Kotler was even more intense.

There are few things that made as profound an impression on me as this. I saw Dad in a more expanded light, as a person who deeply valued Torah greatness and who deeply venerated sages, embracing them, in faith, as family.

That was the real person. But there was more to the person. My father loved pranks, kosher pranks, of course. He had a vibrant spirit, and he shared it liberally. In the mid-1980s, my first wife Naomi (of blessed memory) and I went to Israel with our children for a sabbatical. My father was already there, excited about living in Jerusalem, and always delighted to share that excitement with family and friends, whom he would take to see the sights.

For my father, the reality that because he was in Israel, he had to observe only one Passover *Seder* (the lengthy meal detailing the exodus story) was a great fulfillment; not because he did not want an extra *Seder*, but because it meant he had "arrived," that he was truly at home. (According to Jewish law, Jews who make Israel their home are obligated to conduct the *Seder* only on the first night of Passover, whereas those who reside permanently outside of Israel, including visitors, are obligated to conduct Seders on the first two nights.)

We, who were there only temporarily, did the second *Seder* in our rented apartment in a neighborhood that was more than an ordinary walk from my parents' home.

Imagine our surprise when there was a knock on our door at around 10 PM, and who should be there? My father. He came by cab (he was allowed to drive, we were not), and offered to manipulate the oven and do any other thing that was problematic for us, since for us it was a full holy day and for my father it was not.

You could see the mischief in his eye, but also the glow. He loved pleasant surprises.

My children recall yet another Passover-related incident. We were all together with my parents for Passover in Ottawa. At the conclusion of this festive time, the hectic clean up began. Imagine the surprise on the faces of his grandchildren, when they saw my father vacuuming the floor. "Zaydee [Yiddish for grandfather], why are you doing this?" they asked. Out of deference to my father, they would never have allowed him to do this.

"Well," said my father, "I heard someone say that the floor needed a vacuuming, and everyone else was busy with other cleaning, so I decided to do it." And there was no mischief in his eyes about this. He was serious. For as long as I can remember, every Saturday night in Jerusalem, Dad would insist on helping with the cleanup, doing the dishes and whatever else was necessary.

There was a palpable feeling of mutual appreciation between my parents. At mealtime, Mom would load up the table, Dad would be full of compliments about the food, and Mom would be aglow in the atmosphere of praise.

My mother knew in advance that every *cholent* (traditional hot stew of meat, beans, and potatoes cooked from well in advance of Friday night and remaining on the stove until Sabbath lunch) would be the object of the never-failing comment of my father, "This is your best cholent ever." No Sabbath at home went by without my father rendering this culinary verdict.

This was a basic staple of the family folklore. The only surprise was in the timing. At times, Dad would "pull a fast one" and render the verdict even before the cholent came to the table. It was always expected, but always fun.

Not By The Clock

My father was not a clock-watcher. When you met with him, he had all the time in the world for you, for matters large and small. He was always on the go, but when it came to people, never in a hurry.

When he did something, he did it with his entire being, never going halfway. Thus it was with meetings, thus it was with everything else. I remember to this day how he would fill in a *ketubah* (marriage contract) with such meticulous attention to neatness and clarity. The slightest deviation from what he thought was a perfect product was reason enough to discard the present document and start afresh. He was always so demanding of himself, never settling for good enough. It had to be excellent.

He knew everyone by name and remembered all the details of their lives that they shared with him. They shared because they sensed that my father cared about them, which he showed by always going beyond the perfunctory "Hello, how are you?" His memory was a direct reflection of how much he was interested in people.

As passionate as he was, he never imposed his views on others. He was at home with people of all political and religious persuasions. At the special memorial gathering to celebrate my father's life, one of the rabbis who spoke, Rabbi Berel Wein, mentioned that you could not tell where my father stood, just from seeing the wide range of people whom he befriended. They came from all walks of life and covered the full range of the political and religious spectrum. Rabbis from other denominations came to his Talmud classes, and loved these classes.

My father's *shul* was strictly Orthodox, but the people within the *shul* ran the entire gamut, and everyone felt welcome and even at home. Whatever passion fueled my father's beliefs was secondary to the passion with which he engaged people.

Everywhere I go, I meet people who remember my parents, how my parents embraced them without any pre-conditions. These people, in turn, embraced Judaism more fully thanks to my parents. Many of the children of these people are completely committed Jews, including a significant number who have moved to Israel.

My father had a genuine respect for people. A clear indication of this is the way he guarded their time. He taught by a strict rule. His classes started on time and ended on time. They started on time to be fair to those who came on time. And they ended on time in case one of the students made arrangements to be somewhere else based on when the class would end.

My father valued the time of others, yet there was no limit to the time he would spend for his students. Every question from them received a full and respectful answer. If my father was not one hundred percent sure of the answer, he would ask for a few days to research it. He never pretended to know, and never gave a vague response. And when he came back, it was usually with a small lecture on the topic of concern.

During prayer services, when everyone is reciting the *amidah* (the relatively long prayer that people say silently at their own pace), it is traditional for the one leading the services to wait until the rabbi of the congregation finishes before continuing with the rest of the services.

At a grandson's *berit* (covenant)

When Dad came to Ottawa for his many visits, I would ask the leader not to wait for me, but to wait for my father. Generally, my father took longer to complete the *amidah*, a reflection of his greater fervency. It took only once for him to speed up the *amidah,* so that the congregation would not wait for him. That time was when he realized that I had instructed the prayer leader to start the repetition only after my father had finished.

He wanted the congregation to wait for me, not for him. Much as I would hurry to finish the *amidah* earlier than my father, he was always done before me. He was so careful with the honor that he thought should go to others, he refused to do anything to compromise on this and for that reason was even prepared to speed up his own prayers.

My father was deeply religious, and also very to the point. He hated *shtick,* show-off pieces of additional religiosity that were not part of the basic tradition. This included even the most well-intentioned additions that were clearly super-impositions. When some unappointed person in Jerusalem decided it was a good idea to add an extra Psalm or two to the daily morning prayers, my father protested in his own private way, by not joining in for the Psalms recitation.

My father loved Psalms but hated having this imposed on the congregation, as if this was now the new norm for prayer. The motivation was undoubtedly pure, but that was not the point. Everyone can and should recite Psalms, on their own time, but no one has the authority to unilaterally add this to the list of required prayers. Such intervention he felt to be unacceptable.

As much as he carried himself with dignity and modesty, my father could not escape from being treated with the great honor he had earned but never sought. He would come into a synagogue to pray and never venture beyond the back rows. He refused to go to the front. But wherever he went, he would be pushed to the front. Most of the time he resisted and prevailed, but I must admit that sometimes the insistence of those in charge was too overpowering, and he relented, so as to avoid a scene.

Once, one of the greatest luminaries in Jerusalem, the legendary sage Rav Shlomo Schwadron, entered the *shul* for evening services. My father, who had arrived earlier, stood up for this venerable sage as a sign of the great respect that is thereby accorded to people of Rabbi Schwadron's station. The resulting scene was most memorable.

Rabbi Schwadron reacted in shock to my father's show of respect and deference. "Ihr shteyt oif far mir?! Ihr shteyt oif far mir?! Ihr shteyt oif far mir?!" *You* are standing up for me?! *You* are standing up for me?! *You* are standing up for me?! The unspoken text was—I should be standing up for you, not you for me.

Those who were there say my father was visibly shaken. The great sage had let out the secret of my father's greatness, and my father was emotionally jostled to the core.

We, however, are not shaken. We are inspired.

Memorable Phone Calls

"Nothing," I heard Dad say. Then silence. "Nothing." After another pause, "I have no fee." Again a pause. "There is no fee." This give and *no-take* went on for a few more exchanges. Finally, there was resignation on the other side.

I can only piece together the other side of the conversation from what I heard on my father's side. I dared not ask Dad about what happened since I was pretending I was not listening.

In this conversation, what stands out is the tail end of the communication.

My father was obviously approached to do something. I frankly do not know whether it was a wedding, or a funeral, or whatever. It did not make a difference. He never had a fee for anything. He just went about doing good deeds for others without desire for recompense.

In the end of this attempt to have my father buckle, it was the other side that gave up. Perhaps they insisted on a fee because they were afraid to be sent a massive bill afterwards. They could not get their heads around the idea that there was truly no charge and no hidden cost. With my father, there was none of either. The passion to do what needed to be done was enough motivation.

Indeed, when we went through Dad's files, we found many checks from people who sent tokens of appreciation. Checks in smaller amounts, such as two and five dollars, and checks in larger amounts, including one for $200 (a very large sum in 1974), were never cashed.

Another call that stands out was much more painful to hear. Dad was screaming at the top of his lungs, as upset and angry as I have ever seen him. In those times, rabbis like my father fought many battles, battles which made the work of a rabbi more manageable for the generation of rabbis who followed.

One battle was with funeral directors. In this instance, a funeral director, in order to save on costs, compromised on the meticulous preparation that is mandated prior to burial.

My father laced into him mercilessly. How dare he play around with the dignity of the departed! How dare he engage in such fraud! It was clear from the ongoing dialogue that the director on the other end was trying to excuse himself by saying that what he did was standard practice. My father would have nothing of it. He threatened to expose this fraud, and this director. The conversation ended with my father accepting the director's apology combined with the promise he would never repeat this outrage.

This conversation stands out because it was such a rare burst of anger from a man whose conversations were always congenial. My father's passion for justice and propriety were unbreakable.

Extraordinary Stories

This story at once illustrates my father's wisdom, his passion, and his caring. It involves a family that had come to my father for him to officiate at a wedding. My father went through the usual due diligence, making sure that there were no problems, such as a previous marriage without a proper divorce.

He was on the verge of agreeing, but there was something that nagged at him. He smelled a rat, but could not locate the rat. He decided to do some more checking and called the lady's place of employment for a character reference. She had provided the number at my father's request because he did not know the couple at all until the request came from them for my father's help with the wedding.

The employer gave my father a glowing recommendation and mentioned in passing that he hoped the rabbi could help the girl, since she had gone through so much in her previous marriage. My father's heart sank. He was visibly shaken.

He called in the couple and voiced his indignation at the stunt they tried to pull on him. They begged for my father's forgiveness, saying that they were motivated by the refusal of the lady's first husband to be cooperative in granting the lady the *get* (Jewish divorce) that she needed in order to remarry. They therefore lied and said she had never before been married, thinking that by fibbing they would avoid a major confrontation and hassle. My father came back at them with even more vigor, saying that as unfortunate as this situation was, they had no right to lie, and no right to put my father into such a compromising position.

My father could have thrown them out and refused any future dealings with them. But that would not have been my father.

After making his point, he asked about the refusing husband and how he could be located. My father went after him and finally succeeded in convincing this lout-of-a-husband to give the *get*.

He then officiated at the wedding for the couple, who lived happily ever after — I think.

The wisdom to detect a fraud and uncover it, the passion to stand up for the truth, the compassion for the couple, and the pursuit of justice in tracking down the husband, all combined in this most remarkable episode.

Rivka once went shopping with Dad in Tel Aviv prior to her son's Bar Mitzvah. She loved Dad's taste, and as always, he was ready to go anywhere he was needed. Imagine my father, the fashion expert!

They shopped till they nearly dropped, and were eager to head back to Jerusalem. As they were crossing Dizengoff, the main street in Tel Aviv, my father was stopped by a gentleman who engaged him in conversation for fifteen minutes.

Rivka was growing more and more impatient, as she was more than tired from the full day of shopping and carrying the shopping bags in the brutal heat. Finally, when the conversation ended, my sister asked, "Who is he?" "I have no idea," Dad responded. "He stopped me, said he had a serious problem, and that I looked like someone who could assist him."

My sister was in awe of my father, at his patience with a total stranger after a draining day. Nothing changed from the early days. Dad had time for everyone, real, quality, un-rushed time. And I am sure he helped the fellow.

One of Rivka's friends, Saul (not his real name), shared with her an eerie experience. Saul went to visit his young daughter in the hospital and was startled to find a stranger, an elderly man, sitting with her. The man had brought a doll, and was patiently and softly conversing with this young girl.

The elderly "stranger" was my father. Rivka had mentioned to Dad in passing that the young daughter of a friend was rushed to the hospital, and she was concerned. That was all Dad needed to hear. Without anyone asking him, he went to a store, bought a doll, and trekked to the hospital to lift up the young girl's spirits. Another unforgettable story in a remarkable life.

In Israel, Dad used to climb steep stairs to reach K'hal Hassidim, a synagogue in the Shaarei Hessed neighborhood where he taught one of his many classes. Negotiating these stairs was impossible in the last while before his passing. So my father's dedicated students arranged for him to give the class in another synagogue, which had no stairs.

My father greatly appreciated this gesture, which allowed him to do what he loved—to teach. But he was uneasy with the arrangement because his class was the first of two back-to-back classes, which were normally given at K'hal Hassidim, and students usually stayed after his class to attend the other class. This was unlikely to happen if the locale changed.

My father refused to accept the change of venue under these conditions. He accepted the arrangement only after he elicited a promise from all those who attended his class that they would go from the new location to the *shul* with the steep stairs for the next class, as was their wont to do. This was an incredible, but for my father not unusual, display of concern for others in ways that went far beyond the norm or the expected.

When one of my nephews came to visit my parents for the first time, he did not know how to find the house. So he asked where was the residence of a distinguished man in the neighborhood. The first person he asked responded, "Oh, you mean *him*," and pointed to my father's house. He did not know my father by name, but he knew that a distinguished person resided at 13 Diskin Street, on the second floor. No wonder.

My father went out of the way in all sorts of ways. Everyone in the high rise knew him because he never entered an elevator without saying hello to the other people in it or without holding the door open for those entering or exiting the building. No kindness was too much for him.

A Vibrant Partner, A Vibrant Partnership

My father was always the first to recognize that whatever achievements he was able to realize were due to the full partnership of my mother in everything he did.

This was more than the obvious fact that my mother's total commitment to raising her children allowed my father to give full-time attention to his rabbinic calling. My mother was a full partner with my father in his rabbinic work.

I never once heard Mom complain to Dad that he was hardly home. Her appreciation of his responsibilities went far beyond absence of complaint. It included her full support and total immersion in the growth of the congregation.

My parents regularly talked about what was happening. And of course, we "didn't hear." Dad always sought and appreciated Mom's insight and advice. When they discussed congregational matters in our presence, they switched to Yiddish, assuming that we did not understand. It was through this tactic that we actually learned Yiddish, although we never let on, lest the stream of information cease to flow through our eager ears.

In those heady days of congregational life in New York, the women's component of the congregation was a vibrant force, at times more vibrant than the men's. Mom was every bit the leader of that group. Those who remember my mother from her formative years in England remember her as a great student and a natural leader. All this she showed quite impressively during the years at the Bronx congregation.

One of the major social challenges during their tenure was the re-settlement of Jews who had come to America from the now defunct Soviet Union. My mother was a magnum force. She was totally absorbed with this challenge and worked incessantly to find homes and furnishings for these newcomers. She brought her boundless energy and unyielding spirit to this endeavor, and was attentive to every detail that needed to be addressed.

What she did as a volunteer was more than a few full-time employees were able to do. Like my father, she sought no accolades. Each successful integration was followed by attention to the next family in waiting, with no time to rest on her laurels. She did this for seven years and was responsible for the successful absorption of hundreds of families, absorption which, in these cases, included finding them jobs to keep them going.

Her dedication to the congregation was equaled by her devotion to my father and to us, her children. She was a master cook and baker. From our house emanated an unceasing supply of *hallah* (braided bread loaves for the Sabbath and Holy Days), chicken soup, potato *kugel*, and her own unique potato *nick* (a mix of all the ingredients that go into potato *kugel*, plus yeast, giving the final product a most exquisite taste), which went out regularly to those in need.

No newcomer or mourner was neglected. Dad was often the one who delivered, but as we got older, we joined the ranks of delivery people.

As far as the food that was in the house, that too moved quickly. For anyone who came, be it a charity collector, a guest for the weekend, or a friend, there was no way to escape Mom's insistence that they partake in what was being served. What was being served? Everything.

At my mother's funeral, I commented that she was one up on the Talmud-time philanthropist known as Kalba Savua. Kalba is close to the Hebrew for dog, *kelev*. Savua literally means "satisfied." The Talmud explains about this gentleman that anyone who came into his house hungry as a dog always left satisfied; hence his name.

My mother did one better than Kalba Savua. Even if one came into the house after having just eaten a full meal, my mother made sure there was room for more to eat.

Those who came had a warm feeling of genuine welcome, that they were doing my mother a favor if they ate and drank. In the Bronx and in Jerusalem, the home, however small, was a hub of activity—people coming, people staying, more people coming. Small gatherings or larger ones, such as the post-wedding *Sheva Berakhot* (Seven Blessings—the name given to the post-wedding gatherings in the week following the wedding), there was room for everyone, at least until midway through the main course. By then, people were getting so full that the room was becoming more cramped!

My mother had a keen sense of what was important. (See her most profound condolence letter in Appendix B.) She once came to take care of her grandchildren following the birth of a granddaughter, wearing a beautiful dress with a pillbox hat atop the traditional wig hair covering called *sheitel*. To the question, "Why are you dressed so fancy?" she responded, "Today is a *Yomtov* (literally, a good day, but referring to the sacred days of the Jewish calendar year), I have a new granddaughter."

My mother and father were always available to take care of the grandchildren if the children were away, be it for a hospital stay for childbirth, for a wedding, or for a vacation. On one such occasion, my father helped one of the grandchildren prepare for a Berakhah contest, in which one needed to know the appropriate *berakhah* (blessing) for different types of food. My mother dressed her contestant granddaughter in a green velvet dress and Sabbath-worthy shoes. She said this was a most important event and it was therefore proper to dress accordingly.

Grandchildren coming to Israel to study for a year were greeted at the airport by my parents with flowers and effervescence. No matter where the dormitory was, my parents' home was where the meal was, any day, any time.

Life at home was serious, but there were light moments. One that stands out is when my father, a jokester from way back, came home with a salami. He went directly into the kitchen, cut up the salami with a knife used exclusively for dairy foods, and proceeded to dump it into the skillet, which had butter boiling in it. Mom let out a shriek of horror. This was a dreaded prohibition, mixing meat (salami) with dairy (butter), rendering all the food and the skillet prohibited according to Jewish law.

My father then showed my mother the label on the salami. It was a non-meat salami, a vegetarian salami that had just appeared on the grocery shelves, which no one at home was even aware existed. Whew!

When my father started thinking about moving to Israel, a move that, at its root, expressed in tangible terms a love for Israel that was a dominant and ubiquitous theme of his speeches, my mother was not as enthused. Her entire social matrix was New York-based.

Newly wedded parents of Rabbi Reuven Bulka

Yet there was never a murmur expressed. My mother was totally devoted to my father, such that if my father decided to move to the moon, she would have gladly gone along. She probably would have perfected her own unique brand of moon cookies, a variation on the *mohn* (poppy seed) cookies that were always a favorite.

A little while after my parents moved to Israel, my father was approached to go to Moscow to teach members of the community. We were leery, but Dad was positive. Eventually, he went, along with Mom.

They were there together for three months, as a potent team, with both putting in many hours of teaching and counseling. This was not an easy thing to do, at a time when food was scarce and the most basic comforts were not readily available.

My parents were undaunted. The energy they put into these three months, plus the great sacrifices, did not go unrewarded. The reward — for them the ultimate reward — was a revivified Jewishness kindled in the souls of many a Moscovite heretofore denied access to their heritage. A friend of mine who was instrumental in arranging this trip tells me that, for many of my parents' students, the three months together were transformational. This is no surprise to me.

Upon their return to Israel, my parents resumed extending their communal magic, combining teaching and hosting. Theirs was an incredibly open home. Mom made it clear that whenever her grandchildren come to visit, they were to bring along their friends.

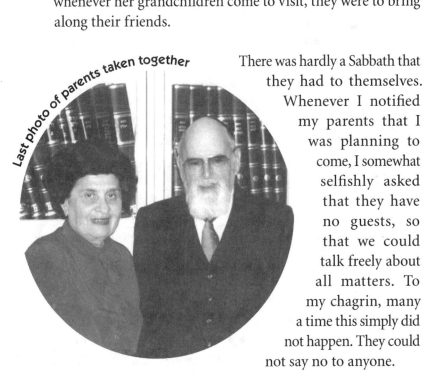

Last photo of parents taken together

There was hardly a Sabbath that they had to themselves. Whenever I notified my parents that I was planning to come, I somewhat selfishly asked that they have no guests, so that we could talk freely about all matters. To my chagrin, many a time this simply did not happen. They could not say no to anyone.

The later years of Mom's life were most difficult. Mini-strokes robbed her of her usual energy and alertness. She was not herself.

Less than two years before she left this world, my father took her to the gigantic *sukkah* (tabernacle) that was built in the square of Jerusalem's City Hall. This was a most luminous sight, with lights that were so amazing that thousands of people came to visit it.

"Hi," a number of ladies yelled out as they came running over to my mother. They remembered how wonderful she was to them when they were teenagers in Jerusalem, attending school and having no family close by. My mother had made them feel at home. They were so excited to see her again and to thank her.

My father came home exuberant at the gratitude that was expressed to my mother. He was brimming with pride for the lady who made his life achievements possible.

My mother hated gifts. She loved to welcome people and wanted nothing in return. Even when we, her children, would bring flowers or wine or trinkets, my mother would protest. It was okay to give gifts to everyone else, but not okay to give *her* anything. It compromised the purity of her kindness. She genuinely preferred that we spend the money on ourselves.

On the other hand, Mom never went to any home or celebration without bringing a gift. In the rabbinate days, every significant occasion in the congregation elicited a gift, be it a silver spoon with the name engraved for a newborn, a wine cup for a Bar Mitzvah boy, or a more fancy gift for a wedding. One of the regular conversation items between my parents was Mom asking Dad when he would be able to go to the East Side of Manhattan to pick up these items.

My mother was an incorrigible (and thank God for that) card sender. She never missed a birthday or anniversary. We had the one-two combination of card and call. The cards were always sent early so that by the time of the call on the day itself, the card had already come.

My mother always sought out couriers to take cards with them overseas and to mail them on the west side of the Atlantic, thereby cutting two weeks off the delivery time. Whenever someone gladly volunteered, Mom "took advantage" of the situation by thoughtfully sending along a full bag of candies "for the trip," for the courier to enjoy. She knew that sucking on candy at take-off and landing helped avoid clogged ear syndrome.

My mother never took anyone else's kindness for granted. She took for granted her own kindness as being nothing special.

My parents were destined never to be materially wealthy. They spread whatever material gain they had onto everyone and were sustained by the tax-free pleasure they gave to others. If they spent money on themselves, it was only for necessities, never for luxuries. And a constant, major budget item was a massive stock of gifts and sweets lest anyone come by, or any situation arise, and they be "unprepared."

Somehow, my mother managed to do all this with the relatively meager income that rabbis earned in those days. We never felt want at home or envious of the bounty that others had. We were full of all we needed, food and care, though not necessarily in that order.

A final comment on my mother's refusal to accept gifts, combined with an insight into her wit, comes from my nephew, who once came over for a Sabbath when he was attending *yeshiva* (religious school) as a teen. Reflective of the caring and appreciate person he is, he came with flowers. Mom got "angry" with him, and he was upset that perhaps he had done something wrong, like buying flowers that were grown during the Sabbatical year and were forbidden for use.

Nothing of the sort. It turned out that my mother was "angry" that he, a young fellow who had very little money, would waste it on flowers and thereby deprive himself of resources to purchase necessary food. "But everyone can use flowers for Sabbath," countered my nephew. Mom, with her usual sharpness (she was quite sharp), responded, "*You* are our flowers!"

My mother's ability to make everyone feel at home extended beyond the culinary. A rabbi recalls the time in his teen years when his train was delayed and he arrived at his home station after the onset of the Sabbath, a serious breach of Jewish law.

He was left with no choice but to go to the house he knew was closest to the train station. This house was my parents' abode.

He came all distraught. My mother welcomed him and made him feel at home. Then, she lifted her eyes upward, asking God, "Please forgive this young man [for desecrating Sabbath] because it was circumstances beyond his control."

To this day, this rabbi recalls how this entreaty put him at ease, such that he was able to enjoy the Sabbath at our home. Mom always had the right words to put people in a positive mind frame. She could feed the soul as well as the body.

In the following pages, you will find the full text of a resolution of the New York State Legislature upon the retirement of my parents. It captures some of the highlights of their career achievements.

Painful Times

The last years of my parents' lives were painful ones—painful for them, and therefore painful for us. In retrospect, they were inspiring ones for the way they fought through the pain with unbending faith. My mother, whose Hebrew name was *Yehudis* (female version of Judah, from which the word Judaism is derived), lived up to that name as an enduring embodiment of *Yahadus* (Jewishness).

Her Jewishness was deeply entrenched in her soul. To the very end, though her mind was compromised by strokes and she had little recall of events and people, she could, and did, recite the entire lengthy *Birkhat HaMazon* (After Meal Thanks) from memory, a truly incredible feat that never ceased to amaze us.

She did the same with other recitations, such as the *Shema* (faith affirmation) recited daily before retiring to sleep.

At the worst of times, when anyone would visit and ask how she was, she would give her usual response, *"Borukh HaShem,* fine" (thank God, fine). She was anything but fine. Her deep-rooted faith contained an appreciation of God for the blessing of life, no matter how much less physically functional her life was.

It was painful to watch the deterioration of a lady (my mother!) so full of life and vigor, so welcoming and embracing. But we were fortunate in that my mother, as my father, remained at home to the very end. They were never institutionalized.

This was not easy to accomplish. We were blessed in the end with dedicated help, most specifically Revi and Mazal, who loved my parents to the core, who cried bitterly when they died.

Even this would not have sufficed in terms of adequate caregiving. There were emotional elements of care that are the singular province of family. The unswerving dedication of my sister, Rivka, who made many a trip with her husband, Rabbi Dr. Israel Rivkin, and also often on her own, to oversee and to help, was of inestimable value.

And we were blessed with the dedication of Rivka's daughter, Tova, who lives in Raanana, Israel, and who made many a trip to Jerusalem to take care of her grandparents. Without her and her most supportive husband, David Kestenbaum, keeping my parents at home would not have been possible.

State of New York
LEGISLATIVE RESOLUTION

Assembly No. 669

By: Mr. Engel

Congratulating Congregation Khal Adath Yeshurun on the occasion of its Seventieth Anniversary and honoring Rabbi and Mrs. Jacob Bulka upon their retirement.

WHEREAS, Congregation Khal Adath Yeshurun has marked seventy years of service to the Bronx and the surrounding communities; and

WHEREAS, Throughout the years, Congregation Khal Adath Yeshurun, formally organized in nineteen hundred thirteen, has made a significant contribution to the Bronx; and

WHEREAS, The beautiful edifice situated on Bryant Avenue held nearly one thousand seats and was an integral part of the past; and

WHEREAS, When it became apparent that the Congregation could no longer function in that neighborhood, the Congregation acquired new grounds in the Pelham Parkway area; and

WHEREAS, In nineteen hundred sixty-two the Congregation began to function in the new area, and in nineteen hundred sixty-five the cornerstone was laid for its new synagogue; in turn, it became the center for many religious and civic activities; and

WHEREAS, The Rabbinical Board of the Bronx maintains its headquarters at this Synagogue, and it is also the center for the absorption of new Russian immigrants; and

WHEREAS, This Shul has maintained an active relationship with the neighborhood; and

WHEREAS, Recently, when the Synagogue celebrated its Seventieth Anniversary, the Shul brought together a large assemblage of present and former congregants from all parts of the world, many of whom occupy important positions in government, Jewish communal life, and industry; and

WHEREAS, For the past thirty-three years Rabbi Jacob Bulka has been the spiritual leader of the Congregation and mainly responsible for the transplant of the Synagogue to Pelham Parkway and its development; and

WHEREAS, Together, Rabbi and Mrs. Bulka are deeply involved in numerous civic and religious organizations, locally and nationally; and

WHEREAS, For a period of seven years, Mrs. Bulka was largely responsible for the absorption of hundreds of families in North-East Bronx, providing them with housing, jobs, and educational guidance; and

WHEREAS, The Synagogue's unyielding commitment to the aspirations and principles of the congregation has so manifestly contributed to the preservation of those treasured ideals of compassion, honor, and concern for others which constitute our American heritage; now, therefore, be it

RESOLVED, That this Legislative Body pause in its deliberations to celebrate seventy years of service by Congregation Khal Adath Yeshurun; and be it further

RESOLVED, That this Legislative Body recognize and joyously commend Rabbi and Mrs. Jacob Bulka upon the occasion of their retirement, wishing them health and happiness throughout their future; and be it further

RESOLVED, That copies of this resolution be transmitted to Rabbi and Mrs Jacob Bulka and to Emil Schwartz, President of Congregation Khal Adath Yeshurun, 2222 Cruger Avenue, Bronx, New York, 10467.

Eliot Engel (signed)
ADOPTED IN ASSEMBLY ON
March 14, 1984

By order of the Assembly,
(Signed)
Catherine A. Carey, Clerk

In the last years, my own son and daughter-in-law, Binyomin and Shira, moved to Jerusalem, and helped my niece in what was always a sacred responsibility and never a burden.

There were also many friends, students, and admirers in Jerusalem, who offered significant help and frequent visits, which eased the care obligations to some degree. And the aforementioned Dr. Doron Spierer, whose office was close by, treated my parents as if they were his parents. God bless them all.

It was not easy to look after our parents, and we were lucky to have been able to head off institutionalization and to ensure for them the highest quality personal and medical care to the very end. One caution that I share with you is that parents and children should think carefully before moving away from one another and creating serious geographic distance. It gives rise to many great challenges, which are not always surmountable in a most acceptable and dignity-preserving way. Dedicated children who are close by offer a manner of caring suffused with love that others are hard-pressed to match.

My father suffered through incredible pain. His mental acuity never left him. Just a few months before he passed away, while we were talking, he chronicled all the things that were hurting him. This was unlike Dad, who hated being a burden and talking about himself.

He suddenly stopped, realized what he was doing, and said, "Enough about me. Let me hear about you. How do *you* think I am doing?" I burst out in uncontrollable laughter, coupled with great delight that my father's sense of humor and precise timing for the unexpected had not left him.

My father had great athletic abilities. A few months prior to this conversation, he could take on anyone in table tennis (ping-pong). But now, he could not walk without pain. And everything else hurt.

The truth is that Dad did not take care of himself. He cared more about others. His heart attack came from the stresses he put on himself. He usually ate on the run and did not allow his body to properly digest his food. He did not purposefully neglect his health. He was just so focused on doing for others that he forgot about himself. This had serious, life-threatening consequences later on. My father had a few close brushes with death, yet he was resilient and always bounced back to his full energy level.

What remains with us is the great dignity with which he battled through the pain, giving classes until the last few weeks of his life. When he could no longer teach, we knew that the pain must have been overwhelming. As much as he suffered, when people came to visit, they could not tell, because he stifled the pain and put his best face forward.

His mental toughness and stoic bravery remain an inspiring memory.

A Mystery Solved

My father came from a book-oriented family. His father was a noted publisher in Nuremberg, Germany.

It is no surprise that Dad loved books. He cherished the books that were published by his father, especially seeing that they were in such short supply owing to the devastation wrought by the Nazis.

My father was an incorrigible collector. When he saw a book he liked, and that was always, he bought it.

Books surrounded him. In his bedroom, books were all around him to his last breath.

My father always wanted to write books. He was enchanted by the books that catalogued the obligations contained in the Torah, the affirmations and the prohibitions. He wanted to write on that. He thought of writing a book about all the street names of Jerusalem, with a commentary giving their meaning and historical significance.

He also wanted to do a book of collected speeches, the speeches that he wrote down on Saturday night after the Sabbath delivery. These are the same speeches that were preceded by his famous mantra: "I really have nothing to say." We were ready to work on this, but were introduced to the futility of the task when Dad admitted that he could not make out his own abbreviated notes of those speeches.

Our family has been hard-pressed to explain why this man of letters, this book hound, this book lover, this most literate person, in the end wrote no book.

In going over the fullness of his life, the answer comes through quite clearly. He started many books, but did not get beyond a few pages. The reason is that he did not have the time to do a book. He was too devoted to his family and friends. He dropped everything to attend a wedding, to marry off all his grandchildren, to make time for someone who needed his counsel.

I think that he was afraid to get too deep into a book, because he would then get caught up in it and seal himself off from the people whom he loved and who needed his time. The focus of his life was people, and he allowed nothing to get in the way of this unshakable commitment.

Chapter Four

Reflections On Mourning

There was a new, and scary, sensation that overcame me after the passing of both my parents.

For a while, I could not pinpoint the exact nature of the sensation, but after some deep probing, I think I finally realized what it was. Even now, a considerable time later, I am reluctant to articulate the sensation, but beating around the bush does no one any favor.

Death is never pleasant. Nevertheless, not all deaths are the same. The death of someone young usually hits harder than the death of an older person. We have greater difficulty when the specific death does not fit the pattern of the older generation making way for the younger generation. When the apple cart is turned upside down, we are forced to deal not only with death, but also with the shock and the seeming unfairness of the tragedy.

We know that we are not immortal and have, to a greater or lesser degree, integrated into our sane and sober thinking the fact that we will eventually pass on.

Humanity has lived with this unavoidable reality throughout history, even though there are recorded instances of people who were unwilling to face their mortality, or others who sought to avoid death by finding a "fountain of youth" or some other elixir that extended life into forever-dom.

We can live with the reality of death. Children who have even just one parent feel the somewhat fragile protection of being in the younger generation. When both parents die, the children suddenly become the older generation.

When this occurs at a younger age, the sensation may be different. But at an older age, the death of both parents brings with it the harsh reality that, at least theoretically, "you are next."

I think this is what hit me at the time, and it was more a wake-up call than a cause to sink into self-pity.

Undoubtedly, different people react in their own unique way to life's challenges. Within a certain range, the reactions are normal and understandable. Some, even at an advanced age, may feel orphaned at the death of a parent. Others, even at a young age, may sense the death of parents as a wake-up call, or as a combination of the two sensations. One's internal make-up, as well as the nature of the relationship with one's parents, and the circumstances surrounding the passing, all factor into how one reacts.

These variables will all become clear in the ensuing pages. My own reaction, while not unusual, is definitely not the only legitimate reaction.

As a wake-up call, I was hit with a reality that should have always been obvious—that life on this planet is limited. This limitation speaks loudly to a sacred obligation to take life seriously, not to squander it on silliness, to make the most of whatever time is left, and in my instance, to learn from the lives my parents lived how to better live mine.

Different Kinds Of Mourning

Usually, mourning does not go on forever. In Judaism, we have some general formulations for how the mourning should unfold. The period between death and burial, which is referred to as *aninut,* is a time when emotions are clouded, when the focus is on making proper funeral arrangements, and when according to Jewish law most religious obligations are suspended.

The day of the funeral is the most intense day of grief. The first three days are "crying" days; together, the first seven are mourning days. The eighth to the thirtieth day are sad but less mournful.

These are guideposts, offering a general framework. Some mourners may fit squarely into that framework, others may deviate somewhat. When the intense mourning lasts for much longer than the suggested norm, this is usually a signal that other forces are at work, that there is a potentially serious problem lurking under the surface.

Just as each person mourns differently, so does each person mourn differently for different family members, and at different times in their lives.

I also suspect that the way of burial in Israel is so direct that it forces mourners to meet death head-on. There is no room to escape from reality. There is no coffin, just a cloth that covers the deceased. There is no dressing-up of the funeral as if the person is still alive or cannot be seen. The reality stares at you, and you have to deal with it.

Before the death of my parents, I suffered the loss of my son and my wife, Naomi. Our son Efrayim died suddenly, at the age of two months, from what is called SIDS, short for Sudden Infant Death Syndrome. To this day, we do not know why he died. SIDS is not a cause; it is a label for unexplained death for causes unknown.

Naomi battled cancer heroically for a number of years. She never succumbed to cancer; cancer overpowered her, but she died fighting.

Frankly, I hate analyzing or gauging my emotions, but I know within me that the crying for these deaths was different from the crying after the death of my parents. The death of my son was an overwhelming shock of such enormity that, even as I write about it now, more than twenty-five years later, I shudder at the image of his lifeless body that remains indelibly imprinted in my thoughts. The grief at his passing was colossal.

When Naomi passed away, it seemed like the world of our family had collapsed. The intensity of the love that my children shared with her was matched by the intensity of the grief they felt at her passing. I am sure that, at the time, I cried as much for my children as I did for the loss I felt for my life-partner.

When my parents passed away, the grieving was palpable, although admittedly not nearly as intense as when I grieved for my son and my wife. I asked myself why this was so. Did it reflect on a deficit in my relationship with my parents? It was a serious issue for me.

I know that as human beings, we are capable of denial, denial even in the face of clear facts. So, I tried to analyze my feelings in full awareness of the possibility that I was denying something, but hard as I tried, I could not explain my less intense mourning along those lines.

I was far from the perfect child, but the relationship I had with my parents, though probably different from that of other parent-child relationships, was fundamentally solid. I could have been a better son, but then, who can claim to be so good that it was not possible to be better?

Perhaps my not crying was because the last days for both my parents were not pleasant ones. They were filled with agony and suffering. However, so were the last days of my late wife. Perhaps it was the suffering coupled with the awareness that both parents had lived full and fulfilling lives.

These answers still left me seeking a better explanation, a better understanding.

A Child's Comment

The answer to my question—why was the mourning for my parents not so intense—came not from me. It came from one of my children. The answer, in the form of a comment, made a sharp and permanent impression on me.

It also probably brought into sharper focus why this mourning was different.

During one conversation, as we were lamenting the passing of my father, one of my children mentioned the obvious contrast between this loss of a parent, and the loss of a parent this child experienced when less than half my age.

It was not meant to minimize the loss of my father. Nevertheless it did help me to count my blessings that, unlike my own children, I had my parents for more than sixty years.

This brought out into the open what I was probably fighting with on the inside—a tension between sadness at the passing of my dear father and a gratitude for having my father for the major part of my life (sixty plus is more than halfway to 120 years, which in Judaism is the proverbial full life).

From the moment of this most insightful exchange, it became impossible for me to cry in sadness at the passing of my father or my mother.

There is a large void in our family, a void that will always remain, because no one can replace my parents as parents or as grandparents or as great-grandparents. But they blessed the family in so many ways during their full life that it is hard for any sad feeling to intrude on the gratitude.

There are many proponents of the need for people to complete a grieving process, to do grief work over an almost standardized period of time. That may be true for some, and in some circumstances. However, it is not a universal truth for all people at all times. Some can condense the grieving into a shorter period.

Caregivers' Guilt

The reaction of most people to the compound grief, as mentioned, was to commiserate with the difficulty of dealing with two deaths, one after another.

As understandable as this reaction may be, the real difficulties, the really tough times, were earlier on, when the health challenges for both parents had to be faced. It was then that anxieties were at a peak, when activity surrounding health care was most pronounced, when emergency trips to Israel at a moment's notice were not unusual.

The cruel irony of the situation was that after the passing of my parents, all this anxiety was removed and there were no worries about having to drop everything to fly over. The mourning period was the quiet after the storm.

What is cruel about this is that from the perspective of those who look after people in need of critical care, death comes as a relief. This can play horrible mind games with the caregivers, who certainly do not want their loved ones to die, but who find themselves under much less stress after death has occurred.

If you want to know from where derives one of the main sources of guilt following death, it is right here in this caregiving conundrum. Caregivers who suddenly feel relief after death and who are sensitive, caring people, may begin to wonder if there is anything wrong with them that they feel this way. After all, should they not be wallowing in grief?

And if they feel "better" after the passing, does this mean that they did not give their all to the caregiving, that deep down they really wanted all this to go away? These are scary thoughts to juggle at such a delicate time. But if you talk to caregivers, especially close relatives, who are plagued with guilt, do not be surprised if you hear them express such notions.

For professional caregivers, this may be less of a problem; for loved ones it can be a serious problem.

To the caregivers who are wrestling with this issue, they should know that it is entirely possible to be totally immersed in caregiving at the most transcendent level of dedication and to have a sense of relief after the cared-for person dies.

For family, surely there is always more that one could have done; however, this need not translate into debilitating guilt. We do our best and hope for the best. In my own case, I surely would have liked to visit my folks more often, but I am continually buoyed by the memory of the great appreciation expressed by my parents every time I came.

The relief after death is not consciously effected. It comes automatically in the absence of all demands for care. It is a relief that, in a very defined way, reflects on the fullness of the dedication of the caregiver, who feels the relief mainly because of his or her total commitment to caregiving. Were the caregivers nonchalant about caregiving, the period after death would not feel so much less onerous.

Emotionally Spent

There is another component to a more complete understanding of how mourning for my parents unfolded, at least for me.

As I reflected previously, it is uncomfortable for me to be so focused on myself, but I share these ruminations only because of the hope that it will help others in similar, or even not so similar, situations.

Yes, the circumstances of the passing of my parents after a full life, and against the backdrop of Naomi's passing away at a young age, were important factors in what turned out to be a less intense mourning.

There is another factor, an important yet perhaps under-reported component of mourning. This is the "emotional drain" factor.

Emotional drain can heavily affect mourning. We see it with people who have spent lots of time caring for an ailing parent, spouse, or child.

When the cared-for person dies, the caregiver sometimes has literally nothing left and is emotionally drained. These caregivers will sometimes fast-forward through the mourning on automatic pilot, neither shedding a tear nor feeling intense sadness.

Perhaps it is because they are relieved that the loved one is no longer suffering. Perhaps it is because there is no more anxiety about sleepless nights, changing medications, heavy breathing, and other problems that continually were surfacing and are now gone.

Perhaps it is because the bank of emotions is overdrawn and there is nothing remaining. One can feel sadness on an intellectual level, but be unable to cry because the spark to kindle the crying is lacking.

This emotional disconnect is present in more mourning situations than we are prepared to admit. Still, we need to understand and appreciate this possibility.

This type of emotional drain can occur in another significant circumstance, when the grief follows other grief.

A person who has lost a treasured child to a drunk driver on the day before the child was to marry, or the day before that child was to become a parent, will be brokenhearted in a way that defies verbal description.

When, later on, the person's parent passes away, it will often be hard to feel as broken up, even though without the previous grief, the grieving for the deceased parent would have been more intense.

Having cried bitterly once before can make it more difficult to do so again. There is no doubt in my mind, and heart, that this was at work in my own situation. The grief experienced at the passing of my son and wife was heavy and intense. There was an internal block that made it difficult to again reach that level of despair. It is painful to acknowledge this, yet important to do so.

As human beings, we are all colored by our experiences, coupled with who we are. This creates the likelihood of a wide range of responses to critical events. The range of responses does not necessarily reflect on the relationship with the other person involved. There is no need, or purpose, in feeling guilty about this seeming deficit in the level of mourning. It changes nothing about the love and admiration one feels for the deceased.

Another somewhat frightening factor in all this is my profession. I am a rabbi, privileged to serve a great community in Ottawa, and always trying, though never really succeeding, in emulating my father, whom I consider the quintessential rabbi.

I wonder whether having seen death for so many years, and in so many ways, including the terribly tragic, has affected my emotional function. Is there something in the back of the head that is holding back on the emotions for fear that the continual flow of this sadness will take its toll?

I do know that the day I feel nothing when receiving a call about a member of my congregation having died, is the day I will resign.

Chapter Five

How To Console

eople mean well. They come to visit when a family is sitting through *shiv'ah* (the seven-day period of mourning) to offer condolence and comfort.

The intention is good and carrying out the intention is noble, but delivering on it appropriately is not easy by any stretch. This is because finding the right words to say is most challenging. Invariably, when going through a seven-day period with a steady stream of visitors, one is likely to encounter some silly comments, even purely stupid ones.

These remarks can sometimes be hurtful, so it helps to realize that those making the comments are full of good intentions and would be horrified to learn that something they said was harmful.

So, what I share with you here comes without recriminations to those who made the comments. Instead, the overriding sentiment is that of full appreciation for those who bothered to come and share.

At the same time, my own sharing with you can be of help when inevitably you will be offering comfort to others. We can never be too careful, or too caring. When we care, it behooves us to be careful.

"Now You Are Really An Orphan"

Sometime in the middle of the *shiv'ah* for my mother, which came soon after the *shiv'ah* for my father, someone walked over to me and said what ranks as the least tasteful of all comments I heard: "Now [that your mother too has died] you are really an orphan!"

To say the least, these are not comforting words. The person probably meant well, although what was meant escapes me. Was it that I was only half an orphan when my mother was still alive, and now that she too has passed away, my status is no longer in limbo and has been forever clarified?

Truth be told, I did not feel like an orphan before that remark, nor do I feel like an orphan now. To me, orphanhood is associated with the feeling of being alone, with no one to care for you, and with being disconnected from the world.

A child who loses parents in the teen years, or beforehand, experiences all the very dreaded things that we associate with the term *orphan*. But someone who is over sixty, happily married, with all his children happily married with children of their own, as is the case with me, can hardly be labeled an orphan, even if that is the dictionary definition.

Having parents is nice, having great parents is terrific. Having them for as long as we did is an enormous blessing, a blessing felt even more when experiencing the impact parents have on grandchildren, as we did.

There are tremendous deficits in not having parents, but that is a far cry from feeling like an orphan. I know that my parents are no longer alive, and yet I cannot accept the label of "orphan"—bereft of parents, yes; orphan, no.

Overwhelming

When my father died, there was an explosion of condolence coming from many places, including the vast community of his admirers in Israel and other places where he lived, notably London and New York.

When my mother died a month later, people were stunned. We were not. We had been living in dread of my mother's passing away for a long time, even for longer than the dread concerning my father.

Even as we were sitting through the *shiv'ah* for my father, we were afraid that Mom would not make it through. She was not even consciously aware that her beloved husband had died, and was visibly deteriorating from day to day.

In retrospect, the real surprise is that she held on for as long as she did, not that she died so soon after my father.

So, we were as mentally prepared as one can be for my mother's passing, but few people knew that. It was not something that could be shared, or should have been shared on a public level at the time.

Many people expressed their condolences coupled with how they felt for us in having to deal with this compounded grief. They were really thrown when, the day after the conclusion of the mourning period for my mother, my wife Leah's mother, Mrs. Pearl Rosenbloom, passed away.

Looking back, it was an arduous time, but everyone goes though arduous times in life.

People were shaken and empathetic at the torrent of difficulties we went through. They knew that the day I returned from Israel following the memorial gathering for my father, I had to turn around just a few hours later to return to Israel because, in the words of my mother's doctor, "it is imminent."

Leah, God bless her, came back from heroic duty during the *shiv'ah* for my mother, to face the passing of her own mother the next day.

We deal with these strains. They come, are dealt with, and then are parked in the "experiences" folder. There is nothing gained in contemplating how thirsty one was before drinking some water. We need to move on.

I am not sure how much worse is the passing of parents one after another, if it is worse at all. We are not in control of life or death. We can and should be in some control of how we react to life and death.

"Dealing" with the death of both parents is, in some ways, not that different from dealing with the death of one parent.

And I share with you a comment made by another well-meaning person after the death of my mother: "Your mother did you a favor by dying so soon after your father."

This person could have meant that since you are down in the dumps anyway, you can handle this better than if the death came much later after the conclusion of the mourning for your father, and you were in reasonably better spirits. Or, the comment could have reflected on the demands that are placed on the children of deceased parents.

For parents, the prescribed mourning period extends beyond the normal thirty days to a full year. In that time, one refrains (with some exceptions) from attending joyous or musical events. And there is a responsibility to recite the doxology called *kaddish* at every prayer service for the first eleven months following the funeral. That is not easy. Yet it is easier to do this simultaneously rather than one year after another. That may have been what the well-meaning person was referring to.

Objectively, what the person said is true, but it is not something for which one wishes. Yet on an emotional level, mourning for both parents at the same time has a significant upside. After all, they were my parents together, and I loved them together, so mourning for them together has some emotional currency.

And, when contemplating memorials, they will always be memorials for both, which again is most fitting.

Must Have Been So Connected

After the fact, we often try to rationalize what seems hard to digest. So it was with the passing of my parents so close in time to each other.

As you can guess, people offered unsolicited comments about how they must have been so tuned in with each other in life, and therefore they left this world accordingly.

It sounds good, but it is pure speculation. To this day, we do not know, and can never know, whether Mom, who suffered a series of debilitating strokes, which severely compromised her cognition, ever knew that Dad died.

Some people were sure that she knew, but were not sure about how they could be so sure. It is a possibility, and that is all—a possibility.

As to the seemingly poetic, almost simultaneous exit, after hearing references to it a few times, I began to chafe. I wondered why it was grating. So, I started thinking more carefully about this seemingly innocuous remark.

It turns out to be not so innocuous. When you say it to someone who has just suffered a double loss, it may sound comforting. But suppose that sitting with you at this condolence call is someone who has also lost both parents, but the deaths were ten years apart. How is that person to react? Does not the comment that they died together because they were so close together imply that those who die years apart were not that close?

Of course this is not what I meant when I said it, would be the reflex response of anyone who is questioned for making such a comment. Undoubtedly, that is not what was meant. But is the bystander who hears the comment way off-base in interpreting the comment in such a manner?

My feeling is that it is not off-base to think that way, because that is the inevitable conclusion, however unintended, of that remark.

Once you say that a couple died together because they were close, then you suggest that there is a cause-and-effect link between timing of death and closeness in life. Such a statement cannot hold true, and therefore brings little consolation, especially if it is made when it can bring harm and hurt feelings to others.

If a remark cannot stand this basic test, then it should not be made. There are other things to say that are not so presumptuous about the way that God works.

Parenthetically, in the midst of writing this, I read about a respected member of the community who died on the same day that he buried both his parents, who died at the same time. The son was beginning the *shiv'ah*, choked on some food, and could not be revived. It drove home the thought that what we went through, however taxing, paled in significance compared with this triple trauma.

Another comment that I heard, and that too many people (one is too many) offer, was: "Now they are in a better place." The comment is well-intentioned, but it is of little comfort. The mourners lament the fact that the loved one is not here, not where the deceased is destined to go.

It is best to avoid other-worldly speculation and deal with the situation that presents itself within the limited borders of our finite understanding.

The Unspoken Words

Israel is a country that has endured many a trauma over the relatively short time since her reestablishment in 1948. She has been forced to say good-bye to some of her youngest citizens, cruelly murdered in pre-meditated homicide bombings aimed specifically at causing the most harm to the most people, including schoolchildren.

In the midst of the *shiv'ah* mourning period for my mother, a teenage girl was brutally murdered in such an incident.

So, it would not be surprising if Israelis coming to pay a condolence call to a family grieving the loss of a family member who lived well into the ninth decade would do so with a less-than-strong sense of grief.

Most people coming to visit have enough sense not to say — "well, at least he or she lived a full life" — even if it is clearly obvious from their demeanor that they feel this way.

Is there anything wrong with feeling this way? Probably not. Is there anything wrong with bluntly stating this? Definitely yes.

It is one thing to have a quiet perspective on matters. It is another to share this perspective in a way that could negatively affect the aggrieved family.

No one who has lost a loved one takes the attitude that the loved one lived long enough and it was time to go. To be out of pain, perhaps, but to die — never. It is just that there comes a time when the only escape from pain is death.

To hear from others these words — "At least he or she lived a full life" — no matter how well-intended the words, is a painful and disconnecting experience. It trivializes the mourning and makes whoever is in despair feel as if he or she is grieving unnecessarily. It disconnects the mourner from the consoler when the purpose of the visit is primarily to connect.

Many people who have gone through mourning for parents have complained to me about this comment. They claim that such rationalizing is demeaning and undermines their feelings. They believe that the experience of many years together with parents makes separation after death even more difficult, rather than less so.

For those coming to console, it is important to ask themselves: how would you feel if someone made this comment to you? If, as I surmise, you would not like it for yourself, then do not offer it to others.

We were so fortunate to have our parents for as long as we did, in quantity and in quality. We did not need to be told this. When we were told this, we cringed on the inside but were polite on the outside. It was an uncomfortable politeness.

"Was He Sick?"

Without taking a survey, my guess is that at least half the people who interact with those who are in mourning ask the question: was he, or she, sick? It is important for those visiting mourners to know that this happens, because after a while it becomes increasingly difficult for the mourners to answer the same question over and over again.

Some people have told me that they were tempted to leave a message on the phone, and/or a written statement on a display board at the mourning site, detailing what was wrong with the deceased, the cause of death, and any other non-invasive particulars. This way, if the question is asked, all that the mourner needed to do is point the questioner to the information site.

Some mourners actually do welcome the opportunity to share, but even they have limits as to how many times they can do this.

We are, of course, shrinking considerably the range of appropriate words that can and should be used in a house of mourning. This is because mourning is a particularly delicate time. It is a time following a serious loss, coupled with a usually draining period prior to the loss. The mourner is thus often physically and emotionally exhausted.

So, what is the implication of all this? Those coming to visit mourners need to think about what they will say *before* they come calling. Condolence visits challenge all of us to be sensitive and careful with what we say. Once the words come out, they cannot, unlike cars, be recalled. They are out there forever.

It is nice when the mourners themselves are understanding and appreciate the good, but sometimes off-target, intentions. But it is less than fair for visitors to rely on this.

Best Of Intentions

A little while ago, I was invited to spend a full and fulfilling weekend as a scholar-in-residence in a *shul* with whose rabbi I have a particularly close relationship.

We worked closely on choosing the topics for the weekend, but it is to the full and complete credit of the rabbi that one of the talks, on the Sabbath afternoon, was such a draw. He chose a topic that I would never have chosen, but which he was convinced would attract a large audience. I was skeptical, he was right.

The topic he chose was "The Protocols of Mourning and Consolation: What to Say When You Have Nothing to Say."

There was a method to the seeming madness of this choice of topic. A few years earlier, this dear colleague made an out-of-the-way trip to Ottawa to visit when we were mourning the loss of my late wife. As we were conversing, someone else came to visit, a local fellow, who began his visit with the following insightful question, "So, Rabbi, what's it like to be on the other side?" I could see the sense of shock on the face of my colleague. He was stunned by the question. Little did I know that he would remember it years later and propose a lecture based on this incident.

The things that people say to mourners can have telling impact. In my case, I actually wanted to name my books with the words that would have the most impact. When I set out to write a book reflecting on the life and death of my first wife, Naomi, and the mourning period that followed, I tentatively gave the book the title, *What's it Like to be on the Other Side?* My well-meaning publisher did not think this was an accurate enough title and changed it. For this book, my initial choice for its title was *Now You are Really an Orphan*—again a comment made during the course of the mourning period, as elaborated upon at the beginning of this chapter.

After sharing some of my observations concerning the pitfalls of mourning at the Sabbath afternoon lecture, I was not surprised that a number of people came over to share their own recollections of stupid things said by people during the mourning period, in the attempt to offer comfort and solace.

I share with you some of the more memorable ones, if for no other reason than to enable you to avoid them at all costs. Names have been changed to protect the identify of the people involved.

Miriam told of a well-meaning rabbi who attempted to comfort her on the loss of her six-month-old daughter by saying, "She died as a perfect soul, never having had the chance to sin." The rabbi meant well, and truthfully many people in similar circumstances might actually be comforted by this remark. Miriam was not comforted at all, and was in fact upset by the comment. Her reaction is understandable. It is true that the young girl had no opportunity to sin, but she also had no opportunity to do good, and that was the unaddressed, even ignored lament of the grieving family.

I have no doubts about the rabbi's intentions or about the intentions of all who take the trouble to visit with mourners. The problem, and the challenge, is that it takes more than good intentions to be an effective comforter or consoler. Presumptuous comments about the good side of a terrible tragedy are tricky at best, highly damaging at worst.

Flora was hurt by a well-meaning friend during the mourning for her husband. "Not to worry," said the friend, "you are young and pretty, you will soon find someone."

Another in the list of silliest remarks was the comment of a lady, whom we shall call Sarah. Sarah had lost a child in his pre-teen years. Her own tragedy ostensibly made her a natural consoler who could connect on an emotional level.

She offered the following words to a parent whose infant died from SIDS: "At least you did not have the chance to get close to her [like I did with my child, which made my child's death even more painful]."

This may seem to make sense as a gesture of comfort, but it misses the point in a most glaring and disappointing way. It is precisely the lack of opportunity to develop a close relationship with the child that makes the tragedy so painful. It is ridiculous to transmute the source of pain into the basis for consolation.

Another, more obviously silly comment, was that offered by a visitor to a lady of somewhat advanced age, but still sprightly, who was mourning the loss of her husband of many years. "Well," blurted out the visitor, "I guess you will now learn to shop for one." What insight, what sensitivity . . .

You, the reader, have probably heard horror stories of your own. There is no need to belabor the point—saying the right words is a challenge at all times, but most particularly during the mourning period. It is at this time that people are most vulnerable, and wrong words are potentially most harmful.

Unanswerable Questions

Aside from the great unanswerable, ubiquitous question — Why? — there are other unanswerable questions, less philosophical and more down to earth.

The question, "How does it feel to be on the other side?" is one such question. To say that it feels good is ridiculous. How can it feel good? To say that it feels bad is likewise ridiculous, since it suggests that rabbis would rather that others have the tragedies so that they can offer comfort rather than being in need of it.

There are other such questions that make the rounds of mourning visitations. Right at the top is the seemingly innocuous, "How are you doing?" It is the equivalent of the parallel everyday question, "Good morning, how are you?"

The person who takes this question seriously and proceeds with a detailed answer that covers all the body parts and the emotions should not be surprised to find less than a receptive ear from the questioner. Most people mean the question as a polite entrée and are not really interested in the details of how you are. They want to move on.

The person asking this question in the house of mourning is perhaps more interested, but usually not in all the fine points. Here there is also an additional conundrum. There is really no good answer to the question. The mourner who says, "I am fine," probably is not really fine. But for the mourner to enter into the world of emotions and share with the questioner all the feelings of guilt, of anger, of pain—well, the questioner is not that interested and is also not that capable of dealing with all that.

Perhaps the best response to this question is something along the lines of, "I appreciate very much your concern. I am dealing with the situation as best I can," or words to this effect.

The question, "How are you doing?" may be genuinely meant, but it can place the mourner in the uncomfortable position of not knowing what to say. It is certainly not the intent of the visitor to put the mourner in an uncomfortable position. But intended or not, it does create discomfort, discomfort which the well-meaning visitor is forewarned to take into account.

Of course, much depends on who is asking the question. A spouse, a close relative, or a dear friend posing such a question is different from someone not so close asking it. To a close person, one can be more open, and may even *want* to be more open.

What follows are observations from Glen and Saguite Holman, following the death of their daughter. Through the pain that you can actually feel, there is much wisdom that is worthy of being shared. I am grateful to Glen and Saguite for making these thoughts available to you, the caring reader.

Please don't ask me if there was anything else that I could have done but didn't. On more than one occasion during *shiv'ah*, I was asked: "Wasn't there something else you could have done?" What kind of a response are they looking for? "Yes, there was, but we were sick and tired of trying new things. We figured it was her time to go anyway. Sure we have other kids, so why put all your eggs in one basket." *Of course* we did everything we could have done.

Please don't help me by describing the root cause of why this happened to me. It is not helpful and certainly has no basis in *halakhah* (Jewish law) or *hashkafah* (Jewish thought) for you to tell me why my child died. I have heard of people who were told that their child died because they ate *chalav stam* (dairy products not strictly supervised, but fully kosher). I have heard of people who were told that their child died because they called the child by a nickname instead of their full name (*Hezky* instead of *Yehezkel*, for example).

Please don't try to distract me because it makes you feel more comfortable. I recall one fellow, a co-worker, who started talking about work. I mean details. He apologized and I said, "Oh, it is not a problem, don't worry about it." He took that to mean that he should continue.

Please don't judge my reaction. One person was offended since he felt that I wasn't hurting enough.

I was tempted to tell him, "Well, we weren't that close. So it's no big deal." Don't tell anyone that you figured it out with your keen sense of human psychology.

Please allow me to be silent. I have been speaking for hours on end, sometimes repeating myself. I am drained emotionally and physically. Be there to comfort me and if silence is what I need, please respect it.

Please don't ask detailed questions about the illness, death, or accident unless you can tell that I am interested in answering those questions.

Please don't ask how I am doing. I lost my child, how do you think I am doing? But you can ask how I am managing.

Please ask yourself, before speaking, if what you are saying is for your comfort or mine. Many times, well-meaning people say things that are self-serving and do not realize it.

Call Me

People who come to the home where mourners are gathered, or who call, or who connect via electronic communication, have taken the initiative. That is good.

What happens afterward varies, but the parting words do not come so easily. In regular conversation, people end off with standard phrases such as, "I'll talk to you soon"—*soon* being anywhere from tomorrow to never.

In the mourning visit, the most frequent parting comment is, "If you ever need anything, do not hesitate to call." My best advice after years of dealing with people in mourning is simply: do not use this phrase. It means nothing and it is unfair.

What it does is put the mourner in the position of having to ask. That is not a nice thing to do. No one really likes having to ask for anything, especially since one is not sure that the request will be fulfilled. One will then feel doubly upset at having been turned down and having made someone else feel uncomfortable. Added to this is the feeling of being shattered that a person you thought really cared really does not.

A person who really cares will not dump the obligation of reconnecting into the lap of anyone, least of all a mourner. The truly caring person will once again take the initiative after the visit and have a thought-out agenda of helping.

From an unscientific survey of people who have shared their thoughts with me, I can tell you that the "extra mile" gesture is appreciated beyond words. It shows, without saying anything, that the person going the extra mile is a concerned soul who is not locked into a formula for what has to be done to discharge one's social obligations; i.e., making a token call or visit. As much as the pro forma "How are you doing?" question is fraught with complications, a call following the official mourning, to a mourner who has completed the *shiv'ah* period, opening with "I called just to check on how you are doing," is most welcome.

First, the wording of the call avoids the need for a direct answer. Second, and most important, the call comes when the mourner, who had heretofore been (usually) surrounded by a host of people, is now much more alone and sometimes feels almost forgotten.

The attitude of many may be, "well, the mourning is over, so it is back to business as usual," which for too many means caring little about others.

An out-of-the-way gesture goes a long way toward the healing that needs to follow the intense period of grieving. It tells the lonely mourner that he or she is not alone.

Thinking of You

One of the most often invoked phrases that comforters express to mourners is, "I am thinking of you." A variation of this theme is the phrase, "You are in my thoughts."

This is another one of those phrases that sounds good until you try to understand what it means.

What precisely is comforting about knowing that someone is thinking of you? Or that you are in their thoughts?

When you probe to the depths of this phrase, it turns out to be empty. A cynic might even think of this phrase as arrogant, as if to suggest that because I am thinking of you, therefore you should feel good.

We can put aside the allegation of arrogance, but there remains the great mystery about how this phrase ever gained any legitimacy. It would make more sense if this phrase was the preamble to a more detailed sharing of what the thinker is thinking.

For example, here is a suggested conversation entrée: "I have been thinking of you. I have been going over in my mind all that you have gone through and the tremendous stress it has been on you, and have marveled at how you showed such great strength and dignity throughout your ordeal. I am sharing with you my great admiration for the way you have handled this difficult time in your life."

In other words, the "thinking of you" or the "you are in my thoughts" part is only the gateway to a more profound sentiment, whatever that sentiment may be. Just being in someone's thoughts is an empty statement, unless the thoughts are more concretely shared.

Another variation of this theme is the phrase, "My thoughts are with you." That may seem somewhat of an improvement, but begs the question, "Why are only your thoughts with me? Why is not your total being with me?"

This may seem like quibbling with words, but may more accurately reflect an unconscious distancing between comforter and mourner. We sometimes have difficulty finding the right words, or truly connecting on the level of feeling, so we create terminologies that reflect this deficit. Perhaps if we used more direct and connecting phrases, such as "I am with you," or words to that effect, this would create a better bridge toward connection with the mourner.

Long Life

The British have a great phrase that they offer to mourners: Long life. Even though I was born in England, it was only after I was well into life as a rabbi that I picked up on this.

The insight came via a casual remark about someone who was offended when, at a small event marking the anniversary of his father's passing, a "former" friend did not come over to wish "long life." Among the British, that is a serious omission.

Years later, as I reflect on the limited nature of the verbal vocabulary available to the comforters and consolers, I remain most impressed with this British contribution to the endeavor.

True, it is a cliché and, like all clichés, can wear thin and lose any meaningful impact. But, on the other hand, it is a wonderful wish and addresses the mourners in a most profound way. After all, is it not likely that those who have just come face-to-face with death are concerned about their own mortality?

Wishing a mourner long life addresses that unconscious and unexpressed, yet real fear, by simply wishing the opposite of what the mourner fears; specifically, a life shortened by imminent death.

Others have offered an alternative explanation of this phrase. It refers not to the mourners, but to the deceased. The hope is that the deceased is now in the heavenly world, in the afterlife, where indeed there is long life.

Either way, the words are short and to the point, and most helpful. They have a pleasant ring to them, which has to resonate most warmly in the heart of the mourner. But then again, I am British by birth, so maybe I am a bit prejudiced in their favor.

In contrast to "long life," another phrase that makes the mourning rounds, and which actually sounds nice, rings more and more hollow. This is the phrase—"you should know no more sorrow." (The Yiddish phrase—*zolst mer nisht vissen fun kayn tsa'ar*—translates as, "You should no more know of pain.")

Undoubtedly, the roots of the phrase are most laudable. The mourner is in pain, and one wishes that the mourner have no more sorrow. But upon close reflection, this phrase is preposterous. The only way a person can be free from sorrow or pain is to be dead. Sorrow and pain are part of life, inextricably so. Therefore, by wishing a person no more sorrow or pain, we are unintentionally wishing death upon that person. No one means that, but that is what it means.

So, my vote is for *long life*. Or, an alternative statement such as, "I wish you good health, and a life full of good tidings and happy events."

Silence as an Approach

Often, when I share with an audience the complications posed by many of the mantra-like thoughtless phrases that are thrown at mourners, I am asked a most legitimate question.

I introduce my observation by presenting to them two comments shared with me by people who had just concluded their *shiv'ah*.

On one occasion, a person complained to me that someone who had come to visit had the nerve to talk about the weather. "How dare they talk about the weather when I am grieving for the loss of my mother?" I understood the comment and dutifully put it into my mental file.

A few weeks later, and with the comment still fresh in my memory bank, another person approached me. "What right did that person have to talk about my father and thereby pour salt over my still raw wounds?" His complaint was just the opposite—a visitor had the audacity to talk about the deceased.

This brings into sharp focus the daunting task of finding the right words for comforting mourners. It invariably leads to the aforementioned legitimate question: if everything I say is potentially no good, what should I say?

Great question. And the answer is: say nothing! Say nothing? Is it not the obligation of the comforter to offer words of comfort? The answer, surprising as it may sound, is *no*. It is not the obligation of the visitor to offer words of comfort. The visitor's obligation is to comfort, plain and simple.

But how can one comfort without saying anything? Comfort is achieved simply by being there, with the mourner, even in silence.

Everyone would agree that coming and saying nothing is preferable to coming and saying something silly or unwelcome. Of course, the best result is attained by coming and sharing wise thoughts and reflections. But how can one know what is appropriate when every mourner thinks differently?

The answer: through silence, through coming with lips sealed and ears wide open. That is the Jewish protocol, an often-ignored protocol, for mourning visitation. Come there, sit, and listen. The mourner will start talking, and you will then know where the mourner is. You can then respond.

This is the safe, sensitive, and sensible way to be a comforter.

By the way, it became clear to me some time through the mourning for my mother that the institution of comforting mourners is not only for the benefit of the mourners. Those who come to offer comfort also need this dialectic. They often feel a strong desire to help out their family and friends by offering comfort. It is somewhat analogous to the rich person who needs the poor person in order to be kind and charitable.

There is another component, namely the comforter gaining some measure of comfort by being able to extol the deceased to the deceased's family, especially when there is a strong sense of gratitude to the deceased. This was abundantly obvious to us from the unending praise and appreciation accorded to my parents during the mourning for them. This time, they were not able to demur.

Saying the right thing, and avoiding hurtful comments, is not easy. In addition to the observations shared herein, I offer insights from Dr. Henya Shanun-Klein. They are adapted from E. Linn's *I Know How You Feel: Avoiding the Clichés of Grief* (1986), and from *Grief Notes* at www.gilisplace.com.

I am grateful to Dr. Shanun-Klein for her permission to reprint the following material here. I hope that, like the earlier observations of the Holmans, it will reinforce some of the points made in this book.

Here are a few examples of clichés that can be hurtful to a grieving person. There are many more:

1. You are so strong.

2. I admire your courage.

3. Be strong for your _____.

4. I would have died if this happened to me.

5. No sense in crying over spilled milk.

6. I know how you feel.

7. Life goes on.

8. Time will heal.

9. Count your blessings.

10. It was God's will.

11. You are still young. You can have another child/marry again.

12. Only the good die young.

13. God needs him/her more than you do.

14. You still have your memories.

15. You should focus/remember the good times.

16. You should think positive.

17. At least you had a chance to say "good-bye."

18. It's your choice to be angry/depressed/sad.

19. You seem to be stuck in grief. It's not normal.

20. If there's anything I can do, just call me.

21. Get over it.

22. Something must have been wrong already.

23. It's better this way.

24. God called you to His ministry.

25. You are so selfish—you just want them in your life.

26. You didn't want to have a baby now/before Hanukkah anyway.

27. What doesn't kill you, helps you.

28. God didn't give you anything you cannot handle.

29. God has something better for you in store.

30. S/he would have wanted it that way.

31. At least you had your 10 years with her/him.

32. At least you didn't have time to get attached to your baby.

33. This [your grief] will pass.

34. You have your whole life ahead of you.

35. Let it rest.

Here are a few verbal and non-verbal statements that bereaved persons said they found helpful:

1. Be silent.

2. You may talk to me while I'm in pain, just don't try to talk me out of it.

3. Just sit with me. Listen to me. Don't give me advice.

4. Acknowledge my condition.

5. Say: "I'm sorry."

6. Say: "I don't know what to say."

7. Say: "What do you want me to do for you?" (And do it).

8. Refer to the deceased by name.

9. Ask about the deceased: "What kind of a person was s/he?"

10. Ask to see photos of the deceased.

Books That May Help

In addition to these helpful hints, there are also some very useful books. On the issue of a life after death, a topic that may not come up directly but is always in the background, Raymond Moody's *Life After Life* ranks high, as does Brian Weiss' *Many Lives, Many Masters.*

Rabbi Marc Angel's *The Orphaned Adult* is a well-thought out guide for those who have lost a parent. Rabbi Yamin Levy's *Confronting the Loss of a Baby* is an insightful and caring treatise to aid those who have lost a child.

For finding one's way through the Jewish mourning process, Rabbi Maurice Lamm's *The Jewish Way in Death and Mourning* has become a classic. And one could not go wrong with a later addition to this topic area, Rabbi Abner Weiss' *Death and Bereavement: A Halakhic Guide*. Both of these books also deal with life after death and other issues most effectively.

The aforementioned Rabbi Lamm has recently added another volume to this genre, a most eloquent book titled simply, *Consolation*.

Though the list of books on the many dimensions of grief is endless, there is another book worthy of particular mention, as it is an inspiration to overcoming tragedy. That book is Viktor Frankl's *Man's Search for Meaning*.

Food, Food, and More Food

Food is a central concern in mourning, as it is a central concern in life. At the outset of the mourning, we impose upon the community the obligation to feed the mourners. Mourners are prohibited from eating the first meal following the funeral from their own stock, so to speak. The meal must come from the community.

This first meal is called the *se'udat havra'ah*, which is often incorrectly called the condolence meal. It is more accurate to call it the refreshing meal, or the invigorating meal. The sense in this is clear. The mourner is down and out, probably depleted physically as well as emotionally.

The community has an obligation to make sure the mourner does not collapse. The community must feed the mourner, for fear that if the mourner is left alone, he or she may not eat at all. By placing the onus for the first meal on the community, we reinforce the communal obligation for extending care and comfort to the mourner.

What has happened to this well-reasoned approach is nothing short of extraordinary, and not always extraordinarily good. The community of relatives and friends often take up this challenge, not just for the first meal, but for the entire seven-day mourning period. They will coordinate among themselves to ensure that every meal is taken care of.

The intention is laudable. People are often at a loss for what to say. Reading this book will not make that challenge any easier. So, *doing* rather than *saying* is a welcome alternative. Within the realm of doing, nothing is more immediate, more pressing, more necessary, and more appreciated, than food. Up to a point.

In some houses of mourning, one of the major crises, if I can call it that, is the abundance of food. In many homes, there is simply too much food. For mourners who are blessed with large families and a wide circle of friends, all of whom want to help, this can be an overwhelming problem.

"What are we going to do with all this food" becomes a major concern and a diversion. A second refrigerator and a freezer are sometimes not enough. So the food, in order not to become spoiled, has to be sent out, usually to food outlets for the poor. That is a good end result of a problem born of great intentions.

But it is not a full solution, since inevitably when there is an abundance of food, some of it goes to waste. There are other ways to lift up the spirits of the mourners via tangible deeds, such as studying in memory of the deceased or donating to a cause in their memory. These have no waste attached to them and are most welcome. Looking after the food is good, but it is also important to be concerned about the mourner after there is enough food.

Abundance of food is not the only food-related crisis during the mourning and post-mourning periods. In some cases, the pressing concern is the shortage of food. When the breadwinner passes away, this can become a major and ongoing crisis, most pointedly after the conclusion of the seven-day intense mourning, when people are more likely to turn their attention elsewhere and leave the bereaved family on its own.

I wish there were a way to magically send all the extra food to the places where food is in short supply. In the absence of such magic, the only alternative is to be communally alert and sensitive to these situations.

God's Comfort

After all that is said and done to offer solace to a mourner, Jews traditionally exit from the presence of the mourner with the following words: "May the Omnipresent comfort you amidst the other mourners of Zion and Jerusalem." The words in Hebrew are:

המקום ינחם אתכם בתוך שאר אבלי ציון וירושלים
(HaMakom yenahem et'hem b'tokh she'ar avaylay Ziyon
v'Yerushalayim)

With this statement, we accurately acknowledge that human efforts at comforting, nice as they are, pale in comparison to the comfort that is offered by God. God is the ultimate Comforter, and it is via faith that we are extricated from the mourning abyss.

There is unending discussion of the meaning of this phrase, including why we refer here to God as Omnipresent and why mention is made of Zion and Jerusalem.

Omnipresent in Hebrew is *makom,* literally meaning place. God is *The Place* of the world. Being in place with God wherever one goes is a great comforter. After all, the mourner will likely be in many painful places. Places such as the burial plot, the deceased's home, the deceased's favorite spots, the birthday times, the special occasions spent together, all may evoke pain.

So, we wish the mourners that whatever place they may be in, God be there with them. And as if to accentuate the hope that is contained in this phrase, we refer to the mourners for Zion and Jerusalem.

On a national level, we have never given up hope, even when Zion and Jerusalem were desolate. We remained steadfast in our faith in God, and God's promise to us, in the darkest of times. That cannot help but give comfort to the mourner in the mourner's dark time, because in the end personal and communal comfort work hand in hand. You cannot have one without the other.

I have noticed a disturbing trend among those who are well-versed in this phrase as basic to the comforting endeavor. I have heard it often and seen it done to others even more often.

It goes like this. Someone will approach a mourner, either at the mourner's home during the official mourning period, or later at a usually chance encounter, and all they say is: "I came to comfort you," or "I want to fulfill my *mitzvah* (obligation) to comfort you. *HaMakom yenahem et'hem b'tokh she'ar avaylay Ziyon v'Yerushalayim.*"

This, of course, is the aforementioned concluding statement of a consoling visit.

That is the sum total of the "dialogue." What was originally intended as the icing on the cake has suddenly become the cake itself. That is terribly wrong.

It reminds me of the woman who complained to her rabbi about the insensitivity of her husband. "I work most of the week, but take off on Friday to create a special ambience for the Sabbath experience. I bake the *hallah*, make fresh *gefilte fish*, prepare a special chicken soup, make the other foods that he likes, including potato *kugel*, vegetable cutlets, mashed potatoes, et cetera, and I also make his favorite desserts. In the free time during the preparation, I clean the house, and make sure that everything is perfectly ready."

"This sounds good to me," said the Rabbi. "What is the problem?" "The problem," said the frustrated wife, "is that after all this, what does my husband do? He thanks God for the delicious meal."

The woman was of course referring to the sacred tradition of reciting the After Meal Thanks to God after eating. There is nothing wrong, and everything right, with expressing such thanks. But there is nothing right and everything wrong if that is the only thanks that are offered. The after meal gratitude must perforce acknowledge everyone who helped prepare the meal.

We recognize that after all the immediate thanks, all this would not be possible without the real Provider, God. So we top off the thanks with our appreciation to God as the source of all sustenance. But such thanks were never intended to pre-empt thanks to those who worked hard, or just simply worked, to prepare and present the meal.

The same is true with offering comfort to mourners. The hope that God will comfort was never intended to pre-empt the obligation to do our level best to bring solace to the mourner. It is only *after* having done our best with that, that we conclude with invoking God.

Like everything else in life, we are partners, albeit minority partners, with God. We need to actualize our human obligations, and leave the rest to God, but never to thrust everything on God. Doing that is a most unwelcome distortion of faith.

On The Fly

We are all busy. There are so many things we would like to do, but do not get around to doing. We know many people. So, it is difficult to go to every house of mourning to make condolence calls. We would like to, but things come up, the time that it takes to get there and back is simply not available, or, in the pressure of time, we simply forget.

What happens is that we resort to what I call "condolence on the fly." We chance upon the mourner at a gathering and rush over to offer a delayed condolence. Never mind that you may be doing a disservice to the mourner by dumping your words when the mourner may be in a different mind space.

Many a mourner has expressed real hurt at being pounced on in awkward places, such as the grocery store when in the midst of shopping, by a well-meaning but not necessarily well-thinking person. I can readily relate to this, as it has happened to me on numerous occasions.

That person should have called, did not call, and now, seeing a convenient opportunity, blurts out a condolence formula to someone who was trying to shop, and instead is brought sharply back to the world of melancholy.

What irks many mourners is not only the dumping, but also the excuse that is offered for not comforting at the time when it was most appropriate. "I have been meaning to call you" is the most often used lame excuse.

Take it from someone who has spoken to thousands of mourners. They do not appreciate this. If you are serious about comforting, go out of your way a little, either by a visit, or a phone call, or a card, or an e-mail, to show some initiative.

A by-the-way, or on-the-fly gesture, rings hollow and often evokes angry feelings inside the mourner, feelings that most often go unexpressed. This gesture hurts most when the relationship between the mourner and the comforter was close enough that a more forthcoming expression was to be expected. This is true especially in cases that when the shoe was on the other foot, when the would-be comforter was a mourner, the present mourner went out of the way to offer comfort.

So, if you know that you will eventually see the person whom you want to comfort, do not wait for the easy moment. It is not fair to the mourner and not fair to whatever relationship you want to maintain with the mourner, hopefully a good one.

Ultimate Purpose

I have left to now an important discussion on this most delicate endeavor to comfort mourners.

What precisely is the purpose of comforting? What do we want to achieve? What should we want to achieve?

You may think that you have the correct answer to the question, until you begin to articulate your answer. You then begin to realize that it is not so obvious, that the purpose is not so clear.

You may resort to the age-old avoidance response—I am going to fulfill my religious duty to comfort the mourner. This sounds like a great answer, but it is a non-answer. If you do not know what must be achieved when you visit the mourner, then you have no clue about the exact purpose of your religious duty, and therefore you are on the way to doing something that is, at best, a rote exercise, and, at worst, may cause more harm than good.

The first thing any would-be comforter needs to know is that this attempt to comfort is not about you. It is about the bereaved. Lest you think this is obvious, think about some of the common phrases employed in regard to the visit. "I must go visit so-and-so," "I do not know what I am going to say when I get there," and so on.

All these statements are "I" statements, which is the wrong way to start. Mourning is about the other, the mourner, not about I.

So, let's switch the focus and pose another question, with a preamble. We know that someone who is hungry needs food, that someone who is thirsty needs drink, that someone who is tired needs sleep, that someone who is cold needs a blanket, et cetera. What does a mourner need?

If we begin with the logical premise that a mourner feels lousy, then we can move from there to the conclusion that the mourner needs to be "un-lousied." This does not mean that the mourner needs to jump for joy. That is unrealistic and unwise, if for no other reason than that the mourner will feel even lousier by having jumped for joy, instead of being appropriately in the moment.

What it means is that the mourner, who is down in the dumps, needs to be lifted up from the dumps, in small, measured doses, to start the journey from grief to gratitude.

How is that achieved? By saying things to the mourner that will make the mourner feel better, that will even bring a smile to the mourner's face. This is not easy. But, according to the sages who have profoundly probed into the depths of this obligation, that is the essence of the comforting endeavor—to say good things that will bring a smile to the face of the mourner, to bring to the mourner a sense of being pleased, even somewhat content.

What will make the mourner feel better? That is *the* question that precedes, or at least should precede, a visit to the mourner. The answers may be hard to come up with, or you may have many answers.

The more effort that is put into answering this question in advance, the more likely it is that the visitor will really fulfill the religious and social obligation of comforting the mourner. And the more likely, then, that the mourner will be helped along on the way from grief to gratitude.

Comforting Words

Based on the observations of the previous section, one of the most effective sources of comfort is saying nice things about the deceased and about the mourner.

Stories about the deceased, ones of which the bereaved were not aware, are a great source of true comfort, often bringing a smile to the face of the mourner.

Saying nice things to the mourner can also be quite comforting. I was on the way from my parents' home to the airport, just after we concluded the intense mourning for my mother, with a planned stop on the way, as is traditional, at the cemetery. Just as we were about to leave, a visitor, Rabbi Lisker, came by. He thought that there was still time left before the mourners would rise from the mourning.

He apologized for not having come earlier, as he had been ill, and simply did not have the strength to visit until this last morning of mourning for my mother.

We exchanged pleasantries in a rushed, standing position. I was not comfortable rushing this fine rabbi who often filled in for my father when he was overseas and unable to give his Talmud classes. Later on, Rabbi Lisker would fill in when my father was not well enough to teach.

I expressed my deep appreciation for all he had done, and he in turn said something that really made me feel good. He mentioned that he had many conversations with my father and that my father was very proud of me. Often the children are the last to know, but that is better than never knowing.

My father was not quick with compliments. That was his style. Would we have liked to hear nice things? Of course, and we did. But it was not blaring music. Perhaps in the long run it is better that way.

My father wrote the Foreword to the translation and commentary I had done for the *Haggadah* (the main text for the Passover evening), titled *The Haggadah for Pesah, with Translation and Thematic Commentary,* that was embarrassing in its praise. But I could not imagine his ever saying these words directly.

Also, he hardly ever said anything directly about the thirty-some other books I wrote. But he always asked to purchase more copies (of course, we never allowed him to pay) to give to his friends. That was the best accolade one could imagine, preferable to any direct praise.

And when I contemplate that Dad lovingly kept every single manuscript I sent to him for proofreading before publishing—something I only learned when I looked through his files—I realize that indeed he was proud.

Back to Rabbi Lisker. What struck me was that this person gets it, that he knows what the essence of comforting is all about; that is, to make the mourner feel good, full of gratitude rather than full of bitterness. This he achieved in a few quick minutes. It is a great example of the type of exchange that fulfills the obligation we have to the mourner.

Chapter Six

Concluding Thoughts

These days, there is a movement to bring distant Jews closer to their heritage. It is called the *kiruv* (bringing closer) movement. My father, together with my mother, never did what is known as *kiruv* work.

On the other hand, all their lives they brought people closer to their roots. But they never harangued them into submission or rained down heavily on them. They brought them closer by their personal magic, by their irresistible and caring personalities.

In a general sense, my mother mainly nourished the palate, my father nourished the soul.

They set the standard by their example, which people yearned to emulate. One person who visited us during the *shiv'ah* period mentioned that he was inspired to move to Israel by my father; not by what he said, but by what he did. He went on to say that he was so impressed that my father moved to Israel during the prime of his life.

I found that quite typical, but also quite funny, because at the time of the move, Dad was in his mid-sixties, hardly the prime. But for my father, perhaps it was, because he was in his prime even into his eighties, bursting with enthusiasm for life.

My parents are glowing examples of how to live and how to be. Theirs was a standard set that is almost impossible to reach, but try we must. The people who knew my parents, and who were not close to their traditional roots, probably said to themselves, "If this is what Judaism is all about, I want more of it." More of it is what they received.

I mentioned previously that my father did not take care of himself. One of the things he did not give proper attention to was, believe it or not, how to sneeze. My father stifled the sneeze, not a healthful thing to do, keeping the noise of his sneeze down to a minimum. This was a deliberate expression of concern for others, that they not be shocked or disturbed by the noise of the sneeze.

In his sneeze, and in his life, my father showed how much he cared for others. And in her energetic zeal to give, my mother showed how much she cared for others. *God bless you,* my father and mother, just as in your life you blessed all of us, a blessing that keeps on flowing.

In the end, the greatest comfort to all of us is the inspired life my parents lived, all the more appreciated due to the accolades and reminiscences shared with us by the many visitors.

I am full of gratitude.

Rebbetzin Yehudis Bulka 1922-2006

Rabbi Hayyim Yaakov Bulka 1918-2006

❧

"It's only when we truly know and understand that we have a limited time on earth—and that we have no way of knowing when our time is up, we will then begin to live each day to the fullest, as if it was the only one we had."

—*Dr. Elisabeth Kübler-Ross*
www.elisabethkublerross.com & www.ekrfoundation.org

Appendix A

Rabbi Hayyim Yaakov Bulka's Farewell Message

to his Congregation before moving to Israel
January 29, 1984

ועשו לי מקדש ושכנתי בתוכם

They shall make a Sanctuary for Me, then I will dwell in
their midst. (Exodus 25, 8)

ואהי להם למקדש מעט

אמר רבי יצחק אלו בתי כנסיות ובתי מדרשות שבבבל

Yet I have been to them as a little sanctuary… (Ezek. XI, 16)

R. Isaac said: This refers to the Synagogues and Houses of
learning in Babylon. (Megilah 29a)

In Babylon after the destruction of the First Temple and later throughout the Diaspora, the *Beth Hakneset* (synagogue) and the *Beth Hamidrash* (study hall) assumed the role of Miniature Temple, constituting the focal point of Jewish communal life. Our own congregation was formally organized in the year 1913 (5674) with the following text as part of the articles of incorporation: ". . . the said Congregation shall keep and maintain, at its principal place of worship, a school for the teaching of children the Hebrew religion, the Talmud and Judaism." It was a tumultuous year for the world at large exploding, in the following year, into World War I. It was also a year of unabated persecution of the Jewish people in Eastern Europe. The year belonged to a period of fifteen years at the beginning of this century, when an average of 900,000 immigrants yearly sailed past the Statue of Liberty toward new personal, political and religious freedom.

As we celebrate our 70th Anniversary there, naturally, comes to one's mind a well-known Talmudic story. Rabbi Choni was walking along, and he saw an old man planting a carob tree. Rabbi Choni was surprised and he said to the man: "Do you know how many years must pass before your carob tree will bear fruit?" "Of course, I know," answered the man, "70 years". "And do you still expect to live for seventy years and eat the fruit of this tree that you are planting?" The planter answered, "No, I do not expect to live that long, but just as I have eaten and enjoyed the carob fruit that my ancestors planted, and I remembered them and blessed them each time, so shall I plant, that my sons and grandsons after me eat the fruit and remember me."

The founders of our Congregation and their contemporaries could hardly have envisioned the flourishing Jewish scene in the U.S.A. as we know it today. Oblivious of some skeptics, who doubted that authentic Judaism can ever grasp roots on American soil, they did what Jews have never neglected to do, to fulfill the commandment: "They shall make a Sanctuary for Me and I will dwell in their midst." The seeds planted in 1913 have yielded a bountiful harvest. Thousands of people have been affected by our synagogues who in turn have made a considerable impact in far flung parts of the world. It has always been the aim of our Congregation to serve not only our immediate constituency but, indeed *Eretz Yisrael* (Land of Israel) and *Klal Yisrael* (People of Israel).

These pages are not designed to chronicle the history of our Congregation. However, any record of its not insignificant contribution to the Jewish community of the Bronx, is bound to include the transplant of our Synagogue from the East Bronx to Pelham Parkway. The rejuvenated Cruger Avenue Synagogue although much smaller than the former beautiful edifice on Bryant Avenue, played a substantial part for the stability of the Pelham Parkway area. At a time when many were persuaded to believe that Pelham Parkway will suffer the fate of the rest of the Bronx, we completely rebuilt and expanded our facilities. Our synagogue became the headquarters of the Rabbinical Board of the Bronx. Under the auspices of the Board, the *Daf Yomi* ("daily page" of the Talmud) is studied daily in our *Beth Hamidrash* (study hall). Under the same auspices the local *eruv* (an enclosure within which carrying objects on the Sabbath is permitted) was constructed with our Synagogue as its central location. The Synagogue is also the center of servicing hundreds of Russian immigrants who were absorbed in our area. A considerable range of all Torah activities in Pelham Parkway, whether of a local or universal nature have always found a home and encouragement in our *Beth Hamidrash* (study hall). The officers of our Congregation and our Ladies Auxiliary can be truly proud of their accomplishments.

It was the privilege of the Rebbetzin and myself to serve the Congregation for a little more than three decades. Let me immediately declare and publicly express gratitude to G-d for being blessed with a Rebbetzin who deserves that title in her own right and whose counsel and utter dedication have been invaluable. ב"ה (Thank God) together we are blessed with our dear children שיחי' (long may they live) who, enthusiastically, involved themselves in many synagogue and communal activities. As we contemplate the years of our association with the Congregation we behold predominantly, a gratifying experience of human interaction in the pursuit of Torah ideals providing us with countless nostalgic memories. However, one cannot help but reflect on the things that should, and often, could have been done. Wherever we have failed the community or any individual we beg for forgiveness. For any achievements, we wish to thank all the wonderful people who gave us their whole-hearted cooperation and to all the officers, past and present, who lent us their unswerving support.

At this stage we look forward to *Aliyah* (immigrating) to our Holy Land. We are humbly grateful for all the good wishes and gracious greetings that have been flowing in. We carry with us prayers for the well-being of all our friends even as we ask for your prayers to be permitted to serve our Torah and our people. We shall always cherish the loyalty and devotion accorded us so generously, and we look forward to a continuing relationship with our Congregation. As long as the Almighty will mercifully grant us strength we shall be ready בע"ה (with

God's help) for any service that may be called for and we are able to render. May G-d bless you all with good health and boundless happiness, with peace upon Israel and the world ע"י ביאת משיח צדקנו בב"א (via the coming of our righteous Messiah speedily in our days, Amen).

❧

"This world is like unto a vestibule before the world to come" (Chapters of the Sages, 4:16).

Appendix B

Rebbetzin Yehudis Bulka's Consolation Letter

to the children of her brother, Max Alt, following his tragic passing in a hit-and-run incident

*The rendition is faithful to the
hand-written original and
has not been edited.*

בס'ד (With God's Help)

מוצאי פסח תשמ'ז (End of Passover, 5747 [1987])

Dearest, dearest and beloved

Trying to concentrate is difficult and finding the right words just as much. Exactly forty-two years after the liberation of the notorious concentration camp Buchenwald, הש'ית (God) took my only and so deeply beloved brother, ע'הש (peace be upon him) from us. Unfortunately there are some words that have become meaningless, such as "genius, צדיק (saint) etc."

because they are just thrown around and someone not even close to it is branded as such. Having been so close emotionally with my brother and having had the זכות (merit) to have known him longer than anybody, I know that he truly was a צדיק (saint) in every sense of the word. No one could ever and under the most trying and horrible circumstances shake his אמונה (faith). On the contrary he, this little man, found the words, the strength and his indefatigable courage to imbue this into others some giants, whom I know and who told us about it years ago. Anybody who has any idea what a concentration camp was like (very little is known to the new generation) knows what it meant to put on תפילין (tefilin or phylacteries) in such a place. Yet he found with הש׳ית (God's) great help a gentle and decent person whom he convinced of what a great deed it would be for this person to hide his תפילין (tefilin or phylacteries), which he managed by a sheer נס (miracle) to smuggle in, not money, which may have come in handy there too, but only his תפילין (tefilin or phylacteries), his most precious possession. This גוי (non-Jew) did it for him and hid them in a little box down in the barracks. Often enough he was sent down by the Nazi beasts to do the atrocious cleaning, he would run joyfully and quickly to put on his תפילין (tefilin or phylacteries) first. Remarkable that they were never caught. You know what it would have meant, instant death, probably the gas chamber immediately or may be with a lot of torture before, if caught. One can only admire this מסירת נפש (life-suspending dedication), courage, ביטחון (trust), love of הש׳ית (God) under all circumstances but the fact that he never revealed this or anything else to anybody shows his character. His modesty, I feel, really was too much, he hardly talked about himself and if confronted with it, he only knew to answer: What a question, why even discuss it, it has to be this way! We both know what a בעל חסד (kind person) and בעל צדקה (charitable person) he was, far more than his meager income allowed. How many people really knew his שכל (clear and straight sense) when asked for an opinion? He put himself in your position and would answer you carefully and logically and many times I sat there thinking what a mind, what perception, what clarity! He knew people, really knew them and it would literally pain him to listen to רכילות (gossip). How could I explain to you, how he treated me when my unforgettable Father ע'ה (peace be upon him) was נפטר (died)! He was indeed my big brother, best friend and always like a Father to me. All we can do now is to be מתפלל (praying) very strongly this his pure and כשרע נשמה (kosher soul) be in גן עדן (paradise) with all the צדיקים (saints) and there to use the access to the רבונו של עולם (Master of the Universe) to be a גוטער בעטער (good intercessor) for all and that משיח צדקנו (our righteous Messiah) should come speedily.

To all of you, his most precious, beloved and admired children and adorable grandchildren, all Rubi, מלכי (Malki), Shabse, Joanie, Guzele and ישראל (Yisroel), how deeply he loved you and how he never forgot to thank הש'ית (God) for these priceless מתנות (gifts). For ever he shall be your guiding light and his total honesty and integrity a shining example, as YOU all always were his pride and joy. How we thank הש'ית (God) for the extra G-d given forty two years after the liberation and how deeply grateful to have been privileged to watch him build such a wonderful family with our precious Paulachen (an endearing way to call the sister-in-law, Paula Alt), may

הש״ית (God) give her a רפואה שלמה (full recovery) to
אי״ה (please God) live עד מאה ועשרים שנה (to hundred
and twenty years) to enjoy true נחת (joyful pride) she so
richly deserves. How good for us to know that there is such
a marvellous continuity and that he lives in all of you. He
never ever wanted to be without Paulachen for a minute and
his wish was granted.

With all our love and admiration, yet with a broken heart,

Yours very loving

Uncle & Auntie

Appendix C

Monuments of Rabbi Hayyim Yaakov and Rebbetzin Yehudis Bulka

<table>
<tr><td style="text-align:center">

פ"נ

עקרת ביתנו

אשת חיל עטרת בעלה

אמנו וסבתנו היקרה והמסורה

הרבנית

יהודית בולקא

ב"ר ראובן פנחס ע"ה

עוז והדר לבושה

ידה מלאה וגדושה

</td><td style="text-align:center">

פ"נ

עטרת ראשנו

בעלי אבינו וסבנו

היקר הדגול והאהוב

מוה"ר

חיים יעקב בולקא

ב"ר יצחק זצ"ל

פה מפיק מרגליות

מנהיג מופלג בדורו

</td></tr>
</table>

Hebrew inscription on Rebbetzin Yehudis Bulka's monument

Hebrew inscription on Rabbi Hayyim Yaakov Bulka's monument

ח‏ן מצא בכל אדם
י‏מיו ושנותיו קידש שם שמים
י‏גע בתורה והרביצה באמריקה ובארה"ק
ם - מוכתר במדות, עניו וצנוע מהותו

י‏וצאי חלציו ממשיכים תורתו ודוגמתו
ע‏מל כל ימיו לטובת הכלל והפרט
ק‏בל כל אדם בשמחה ובאהבה
ב‏ית פתוח לרווחה עם זוגתו הקים

נלב"ע ב' אדר תשס"ו
תנצב"ה

Hebrew name acrostic inscribed on Rabbi Hayyim Yaakov Bulka's monument

י‏ראת שמים היא תהילתה
ה‏כנסת אורחים קיימה בכל לבה
ל‏קהילותיה כבדוה והוקירו חסדיה
ד‏בקה בבעלה ובתורתו באהבה
י‏לדיה נכדיה ויניה האריכו אורח חייה
ת‏וך תוכה מלאה תפילה

Hebrew name acrostic inscribed on Rebbetzin Yehudis Bulka's monument

נלב"ע ב' ניסן תשס"ו
תנצב"ה

More great books

from Paper Spider

25% off
Chicken Soup with Chopsticks

Exclusive offer to owners of
Turning Grief into Gratitude
See last page of this book
for details

Free books for school libraries

See www.PaperSpider.Net/about
for details

Upcoming Title

How to Screen Your Date:
Secret Shortcuts to
Long-term Happiness

Share Your Thoughts

Share your thoughts about *Turning Grief into Gratitude* by posting your comments on these web sites:

www.Amazon.com
www.PaperSpider.Net

or by filling out the form on the next page.

1. *What* do you especially like or dislike about the book's content?

2. *Why?* Please give details.

3. *How* did reading this book affect your awareness or views about the subject matter?

Fax or mail your comments to us

Fax: 613-321-9866

Name	
Profession (& Title)	
City & Country	
Email address	
Phone number	

Submissions become property of Paper Spider and may be used for publicity.

Your comments

Tear

Affix
required
postage

Paper Spider, Readers' Reviews

8 - 1821 Walkley Road,
Room B101, Ottawa,
Ontario, K1H 6X9
Canada

About the Author

Reuven Bulka has been the Rabbi of Congregation Machzikei Hadas in Ottawa, Canada, since 1967, at the age of 23. He obtained a Ph.D. in psychology from University of Ottawa in 1971, specializing in the Logotherapy of Viktor Frankl.

Rabbi Dr. Reuven P. Bulka is the host of the TV series *In Good Faith,* as well as the radio programs *Sunday Night with Rabbi Bulka* (CFRA) and *JEW-BILATION* (CHIN Radio). He authored over 30 books and has been a columnist, editor and writer for over 20 publications. He is a regular columnist for the Ottawa Citizen's *Ask the Religion Experts.*

A dynamic community leader in both religious and secular matters, Rabbi Bulka chairs eight committees, including: Religious and Inter-religious Affairs Committee of Canadian Jewish Congress; Courage Campaign for the Ottawa Regional Cancer Foundation; and Communications Committee — Trillium Gift of Life Network. He is also the recipient of ten prestigious honors and awards, including: Honourary Doctorate of Laws, Carleton University; Bronfman Medal, Canadian Jewish Congress; as well as Canadian Blood Services: Honouring Our Life Blood.

Other books by the Author

(Partial list)

Religion from A to Z. Renfrew: General Store Publishing House, 2006.

The Haggadah Connection. Southfield, Michigan: Targum Press, 2005.

Best Kept Secrets of Judaism. Southfield, Michigan: Targum Press, 2002.

More Answers to Questions of the Spirit. Ottawa, Ontario: Mosaic Press, 2002.

Answers to Questions of the Spirit. Ottawa, Ontario: Mosaic Press, 2000.

Judaism on Illness and Suffering. Northvale, New Jersey: Jason Aronson Publications, 1998.

An Unforgettable Hour: Congregation Machzikei Hadas Receives a Coat of Arms. Ottawa, 1998.

Tefilah v'Tikvah — Prayer and Hope. Hoboken, New Jersey: Ktav Publishing Company, 1997.

The RCA Lifecycle Madrikh. New York: Mesorah Publications, 1995.

Sermonic Wit. Jerusalem: Keren HaYesod, 1995.

More Torah Therapy: Further Reflections on the Weekly Sedra and Special Occasions. Hoboken, N.J.: Ktav Publishing Company, 1993.

More of What You Thought You Knew About Judaism: 354 Misconceptions About Jewish Life. Northvale, N.J.: Jason Aronson, 1993.

Critical Psychological Issues: Judaic Perspectives. Lanham, Maryland: University Press of America, 1992.

Jewish Divorce Ethics: The Right Way to Say Goodbye. Ogdensberg, New York: Ivy League Press, 1992.

Uncommon Sense for Common Problems. Toronto, Ontario: Lugus Productions, 1990.

Individual, Family, Community: Judeo-Psychological Perspectives. Oakville, Ontario: Mosaic Press, 1989.

What You Thought You Knew About Judaism: 341 Common Misconceptions about Jewish Life. Northvale, N.J.: Jason Aronson, 1989.

The Coming Cataclysm: The Orthodox-Reform Rift and the Future of the Jewish People. Oakville, Ontario: Mosaic Press, 1984. Second Edition, 1986.

Jewish Marriage: A Halakhic Ethic. Hoboken, New Jersey: Ktav Publishing Company, 1986.

The Jewish Pleasure Principle. New York: Human Sciences Press, 1986. (Paperback edition, 1989).

Loneliness. Toronto: Guidance Centre of University of Toronto, 1984.

Dimensions of North American Orthodox Judaism (Ed.). New York: Ktav Publishing Company, 1983.

Torah Therapy: Reflections on the Weekly Sedra and Special Occasions. New York: Ktav Publishing Company, 1983.

Holocaust Aftermath: Continuing Impact on the Generations (Ed.). New York: Human Sciences Press, 1981.

As a Tree by the Waters — Pirkey Avoth: Psychological and Philosophical Insights. New York: Feldheim, 1980. Reprinted as part of Jewish Classics Series by Jason Aronson, 1993.

Logotherapy in Action. Co-Editor with Joseph Fabry and William Sahakian. New York: Jason Aronson, 1979.

The Quest for Ultimate Meaning: Principles and Applications of Logotherapy. New York: Philosophical Library, 1979.

Mail in this original order form (see reverse)
as your proof of purchase to qualify
for the exclusive 25% discount

Proof of Purchase

ISBN 978-0-9732523-6-1

Order Form

Title	Qty.	Subtotal (choose US$ or CDN$)
Turning Grief Into Gratitude US$14.95 / CDN$16.95		
25% off *Chicken Soup with Chopsticks* Retail: US$18.18; Discounted: US$13.64 or CDN$22.95; CDN$17.21		

Shipping & handling (First item)
     To US: US$ 8.95 (7 business days, no POB)
          US$ 1.95 (within 12 weeks, POB okay)
     To Canada: CDN$ 8.95
     To UK: US$5.95 or CDN$6.95
     To other countries: US$11.95 or CDN$13.95		

For 2nd item and more:
     Add $1 for each item to Canada, US, and UK;
     or add $4 for other countries		

Sales Tax (for shipment to Canada only)
     6% for AB, BC, MB, NT, NU, ON, PE, QC, SK, YT
     14% for NB, NF, NS		

Total $		

Purchaser Information

☐	Payment enclosed	US$ or CDN$ (US checks, Canadian checks, and money orders accepted)
	Full Name	
	Email Address	
	Daytime Phone no.	
	Shipping Address	
	City, Province/State	
	Postal Code/ZIP	
	Country	

Please mail to: **Paper Spider, Book Order**
                     8-1821 Walkley Road
                     Room B101, Ottawa
                     ON, K1H 6X9 Canada

Tear

Paper Spider ®

www.PaperSpider.Net
Phone 1-888-BOOKS-88

Rabbi Dr. Reuven P. Bulka:

"Reading this book, one cannot but be filled with admiration for their singular attainment."

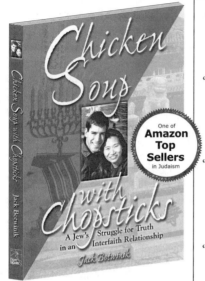

Order: 1-888-BOOKS-88
www.PaperSpider.Net
US$18.18/CDN$22.95

So, what happens when a nice Jewish boy falls in love with a Chinese lady?

"If anyone knows of someone in such a dilemma [interfaith relationship], this book should be required reading."

—*The Jewish Press*

"Anyone who still thinks that Judaism is only for those born Jewish should read this inspiring book."

—*Dennis Prager,*
radio talk show host

"...helpful for couples contemplating interfaith relationships ... a good addition to synagogue and public library collections."

—*Association of Jewish Libraries*

This true story depicts the challenges a Jew is confronted with in dating a Chinese woman, and how this interfaith dating experience leads them both to become committed to Judaism.

Recommended by **Rabbi Michael Skobac** of Jews for Judaism, and **Rabbi Kalman Packouz** of Aish HaTorah

Authored by Jack Botwinik, Dating Columnist for *Ottawa Jewish Bulletin.*

Receive 25% off *Chicken Soup with Chopsticks,* if you already own, or will order, *Turning Grief Into Gratitude.*

Mail in the original order form on previous page to receive this exclusive discount.

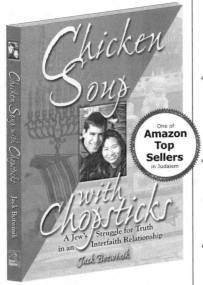